the gender friend

of related interest

They/Them/Their
A Guide to Nonbinary and Genderqueer Identities
Eris Young
ISBN 978 1 78592 483 5
eISBN 978 1 78450 872 2

Everything You Ever Wanted to Know about Trans
(But Were Afraid to Ask)
Brynn Tannehill
ISBN 978 1 78592 826 0
eISBN 978 1 78450 956 9

The Book of Non-Binary Joy
Embracing the Power of You
Ben Pechey
Illustrated by Sam Prentice
ISBN 978 1 78775 910 7
eISBN 978 1 78775 911 4

Trans Power
Own Your Gender
Juno Roche
ISBN 978 1 78775 019 7
eISBN 978 1 78775 020 3

the gender friend

A 102 Guide to Gender Identity

OAKLEY PHOENIX

Foreword by Jackson Bird

Jessica Kingsley Publishers

London and Philadelphia

First published in Great Britain in 2023 by Jessica Kingsley Publishers
An imprint of Hodder & Stoughton Ltd
An Hachette Company

1

A CIP catalogue record for this title is available from the
British Library and the Library of Congress

ISBN 978 1 83997 357 4
eISBN 978 1 83997 358 1

Printed and bound in Great Britain by Clays Ltd

Jessica Kingsley Publishers' policy is to use papers that are natural,
renewable and recyclable products and made from wood grown in
sustainable forests. The logging and manufacturing processes are expected
to conform to the environmental regulations of the country of origin.

Jessica Kingsley Publishers
Carmelite House,
50 Victoria Embankment,
London EC4Y 0DZ

www.jkp.com

To Twig, my cat-in-law.

Contents

Foreword

In one of the earliest entries in *theoaknotes*, when Oakley was still in that electrically-charged period of coming out—when you're buzzing with excitement about moving forward, but weighed down by the worries and questions of others—they wrote, "it gets tiring being the local spokesperson for the nonbinary and trans communities, but I want to be there to support family and friends who have questions. It's a balancing act. I might open up an advice column in the local newspaper and answer all of the questions I receive there. (I wouldn't, but isn't that a dream?)"

They may not have started that advice column per se, but I sometimes think of blogs as the modern-day equivalent to local newspapers, and with how far and wide their subsequent entries ended up spreading, I think it's fair to say that that dream materialized. And now, with this book, Oakley's insights and wisdom will be reaching readers far beyond their local community and corner of the internet.

But I fully understand that desire Oakley expressed.

The ension between wanting to help people understand—both for your own benefit and that of other trans and nonbinary people—but also being just plain exhausted is real. The first round of coming out[1] can be pretty arduous—especially as a trans person. It's not just repeating the same emotionally-vulnerable testimony to each person in your life over and over again—sometimes not knowing whether the other person will support you or not. As a trans person, that conversation is inevitably followed by defining terminology, outlining your transition plans, and maybe even myth-busting some assumptions about basic biology.

That's part of why, when I came out as a man, I posted a twelve-and-a-half minute YouTube video telling my story, sharing my new name, and breaking down some trans basics. Like Oakley did on their blog, I wanted one place to lay it

---

1   I say "first round" because coming out is a lifelong process. Even though many of us have one big, initial coming out, LGBTQIA+ people are tasked with coming out repeatedly throughout our lives—when meeting new friends, when discussing our history with medical providers, when dating. For some people, in some situations, sharing their sexual orientation or gender identity is something they wish to keep private. For others, it's no big deal. And for still others, the option to not be read as LGBTQIA+ doesn't exist. But the reality of continually letting other people in on this personal part of one's identity remains a burden on LGBTQIA+ people until society writ large revises the default assumption that all people they encounter are cisgender and heterosexual until proven otherwise.

all out in my own words, without interruption. I too had told several people in my life at that point, but it's hard to track down every person you've ever met that you might see again one day and schedule a phone call or coffee date with them. And even if you could, after just three or four of those conversations, you start to get pretty worn down. So, for me, with an existing audience on YouTube who needed to be let in on this development anyways, a video seemed like the perfect solution.

I often describe the period around coming out as the one in my life I would least like to relive. While it was enormously gratifying, it was a time of intense highs and very low lows. Every moment, every interaction, every thought was seared with a hyperawareness of the truth I had recently revealed and the new terrain I was embarking on.

For Oakley, that new terrain came with some additional obstacles that I didn't encounter. While trans awareness has accelerated by leaps and bounds since I came out in 2015, a lot of people still get a bit tripped up around nonbinary genders. What exactly does nonbinary mean? Do nonbinary people medically transition? How do you use they/them pronouns?

Whereas I faced the awkwardness and the fear of rejection when explaining to people that I now went by Jack and would be living openly as the man I knew myself to be, Oakley often has to explain how to conjugate they/them pronouns and dispel rude assumptions about nonbinary genders being nothing more than a new trend.[2] There's a lot more educating required in their day-to-day experience so I hope Oakley's blog, and now this book, can help them, and all nonbinary people, be relinquished of that obligation to educate so they can just kick back and be themselves without question or judgment.

That said, if you read those hypothetical questions above and weren't sure how to answer them, that's okay! That's what this book is for. Oakley is an amazing, friendly teacher. This book will help you level up as an ally and even think a bit more deeply about your own gender.

Even though I'm trans myself and have built something of a career around running workshops and making videos about trans experiences, I still found myself being challenged and inspired by Oakley's guidance in the following pages.

I'm a little over ten years older than Oakley, but we do

---

2   Not only could the many nonbinary people in their fifties onward who have identified as such for decades be enough to dispel the myth that being nonbinary is something that was invented by people on the internet a few years ago, but you could look back at almost any culture throughout time and find people who transcended gender bounds in one way or another. In many cultures, such people were celebrated or at least considered just as ordinary and respected as any other person—at least until other cultures with more binary immutable ideas about gender invaded, stamping out other forms of gender expression and identity and doing their best to erase those people's stories from the historical records. As we have shown time and time again, however, we cannot be erased.

have a number of things in common. We were brought up at least partially in pretty gendered environments—Catholic school in a small town for Oakley; Dallas' the-bigger-the-hair-the-closer-to-God culture for me. Neither of us was really exposed to the full breadth of options available to us for gender expression and identity until college. Reading about Oakley's whirlwind process of discovery and exploration as a freshman mirrored the breakneck speed with which I dove into researching trans topics as soon as I finally learned the words to describe how I'd been feeling all my life.

But unlike Oakley, I didn't share that realization with people in my life or begin socially or medically transitioning for many years to come. I wasn't ready yet. I had a lot of baggage to work through, and I didn't have trans or nonbinary peers I could confide in or who could help me find the resources I needed.

And that's okay. For some of us, it takes a little longer. As Oakley reminds us "...there is no one-size-fits-all for gender journeys... Every gender journey deserves respect as it occurs on the timeline that works for each individual."

* * *

When I was promoting my first book, *Sorted: Growing Up, Coming Out, and Finding My Place*, I was lucky enough to do a couple of joint events with one of my favorite authors, Alex Myers. A fellow trans person, Alex is about a decade older than me. He was the first openly trans person at both Phillips Exeter Academy and Harvard University, so he's long been accustomed to breaking new ground for subsequent trans people to tread.

Alex's first book was a historical fiction novel called *Revolutionary*. It tells the story of his ancestor, Deborah Sampson, who dressed as a man in order to fight in America's Revolutionary War. As a history buff, I loved Alex's portrayal of queerness and gender nonconformity in a setting more often associated with a traditionally gendered flavor of patriotism. So when Alex's next novel, *Continental Divide*, came out around the same time as my memoir, I was stoked when he agreed to combine book promotion forces.

Continental Divide is about a newly out trans guy in the 1990s who heads out west to work on a ranch in Wyoming. One night, when we were in conversation at an event at Brookline Booksmith in Massachusetts, Alex remarked how, given that his first novel was set in the 18th century, he initially felt like setting *Continental Divide* in the 1990s was downright contemporary. Then, he said, he read my memoir and realized that he was, comparatively, still writing historical fiction. My experiences of coming out via a YouTube video, having to brainstorm a new username and decide whether to scrub the footprints of an entire adolescence documented online was so alien to his experience coming out in 1995 that it made *Continental Divide*, and Alex's own experiences, feel like a period piece.

Reading *The Gender Friend* at times made me feel like my experiences are already hastening towards the historical.

Alex couldn't imagine having to deal with transitioning in the age of social media, but I can't imagine working up the guts to transition without the examples of fellow trans people online to encourage me. And, in the other direction, I can't imagine starting to transition in pandemic-driven isolation like Oakley has done.

As Oakley sagely pointed out once in a blog post about trans elders, our different generations have all had their own challenges. It's not fair to compare them, to start quibbling about who had it the easiest. And that's not even getting into how trans people are all so different from one another in ways that not even generational similarities can unite. It's also not always fair to thrust the responsibility of elder-ship on someone who simply doesn't share the same experiences that the younger generations are grappling with. That would-be elder may not be able to effectively give advice in a landscape so transformed from when they were that age.

So I'll try not to put on a "trans elder" hat here and act like I totally understand what Oakley is going through and have sage advice for them. After all, I have no clue what it's like to start transitioning during a pandemic, or be a Black genderqueer person, or even what it's like to live on the west coast!

But I think we can always learn from conversations with one another. And since Oakley has generously devoted this book to sharing their experiences and expertise with others, I thought I'd end with sharing some of my own with them—not as an elder (because my gosh, I'm only in my early thirties!), just trans person-to-trans person.

Oakley often describes their writing as a Gen Z kid explaining gender to you over a coffee date. In a few chapters, you'll get a chance to go on a coffee date with Oakley yourself. But for now, I'm going to turn the tables and ask them out for a coffee. You're invited to listen in from a nearby table.

[Oakley and I sit down at their favorite local coffee shop. I order them a blended chai and a drip coffee with almond milk for myself.]

ME: Thanks for showing me this place, Oakley! I love checking out new coffee shops.

OAKLEY: My pleasure! I'm glad we're getting a chance to chat—even if it's imaginary and you're making up all the words I'm saying.

ME: You're right. That's not super fair. Maybe I'll do most of the talking for now then?

[Oakley silently gestures for me to take it away, then relaxes back in their seat and takes a sip of their chai.]

ME: I mostly wanted to let you know how much I loved your book, and how much it meant to me. I really admired how carefully you broke everything down and led the readers through thought-provoking exercises instead of just talking at them. Because no one likes just being talked to without getting their own words in, right?

OAKLEY: Y'know, it's funny you should say that—

ME: Anyways, what you said about gender journeys not being fixed or linear and there being something freeing in that really stuck with me. I hope people return to *The Gender Friend* over and over again throughout the years, looking back on their responses to the exercises and seeing how they've grown or changed each time.

[Oakley smiles.]

ME: When I was writing my book, one of the scariest things was knowing that I would grow and change over time, but that the book would remain this time capsule of who I was in 2019. And that people who picked it up years later would only meet me as I was in 2019, not knowing the person I had become since. What I finally had to acknowledge was that just because you might change one day, isn't a reason to not be fully and unapologetically you today. The lightness and curiosity with which you explain gender, Oakley, I think makes it so much less intimidating—and even exciting—for people figuring out their own gender, or trying to understand someone else's. So thank you for this book, Oakley, and for letting me put a few words in your mouth at the start of it.

OAKLEY: Hey, what else could I say? Thanks for taking the time, and for the drink!

[Oakley and I tap our drinks together in cheers, share a few private words, and then invite you to join our table for a lively discussion about gender, Schitt's Creek, the best alternative milks for coffee, and our dreams for a future world in which every person feels safe and celebrated being exactly who they are.]

Jackson Bird
Queens, New York
February 2022

Introduction

Welcome!

Take a deep breath. Close your eyes. Inhale, then exhale. Repeat these steps as many times as you need. We aren't in a rush, and I want you to be in a peaceful headspace as you begin to read. Welcome to *The Gender Friend*. I'm glad to have you here. Before we start, I want to set three intentions:

1. As you read, your thoughts, feelings, and concerns will be acknowledged respectfully. I won't assume that you have any prior experience with gender advocacy, and I will aim to meet you where you're at.

2. In moments where you are called to expand on your understanding of gender, you'll be encouraged to do so at a pace that is comfortable and accessible for you. We are going to ask some big questions, and I don't want you to get overwhelmed.

3. You are welcome and invited to actively engage with this

text. Take notes in the margins, answer the questions that are asked of you, and exchange thoughts with others as you encounter concepts and stories that intrigue you.

If you lifted this book from the shelf, you're interested in learning more about gender. You could be in the earliest stages of questioning, fresh out of the closet, well into your transition, or an ally hoping to receive some tips and tricks to assist you in caring for a loved one in any of the positions I just mentioned. No matter your starting point, you're in the right place. We're going to explore the ins and outs of gender together—covering everything from affirming language and fashion advice to how my mom reacted to me coming out as trans and nonbinary.

My goal is to build a bridge from wherever you are to me, a genderqueer person ready to actively listen, advise you as needed, and provide you with support as you approach the next steps in your own unique gender journey. To my knowledge, there isn't an all-in-one book of this nature yet. This is part workbook, part textbook, part advice column, and part storytelling—all told by a Black, queer, transmasculine, nonbinary young adult. We're going to move through this text together, and by the end of it, you'll be able to say that you intimately know a non-cisgender person. You'll have a "gender friend," if you will. Hi. I'm Oakley. It's nice to meet you. Welcome to the book you've been waiting for.

CHAPTER 1

Who Am I?

As your newly assigned gender friend, I should introduce myself. My name is Oakley. That's me on the right. I'm 20, and I live in the Pacific Northwest. I attend a small, liberal arts institution in northern Oregon where I major in women's and gender studies and minor in English and sociology. I grew up in the Bay Area with my

moms, two interracial lesbians from the 1970s. I run a blog centered around gender and sexuality called *theoaknotes*, and I'm an unofficial gender therapist for nearly everyone in my life. You could say that gender is my full-time job, and you wouldn't be all that wrong.

Outside my life's gender emphasis, I'm not that different from your average 20-year-old. I can be found in coffee shops journaling, writing articles, and catching up with friends, in libraries reading or nodding off in the sunnier corners, or in a gym—shoutout to Catalyst Community Fitness (or "CatFit" for short) for showing me that there is joy to be found in lifting heavy things with other queer people at 6am! I have an undying love for *Schitt's Creek*, *The Chronicles of Narnia*, and BTS. I'm overcommitted and slowly but surely learning how to undo the nightmare that is my Google Calendar. I'm teaching myself how to cook and how to maintain a monthly budget. Like I said, I'm a standard human being in their twenties.

But you're here to get the hang of gender, so let's focus on that. You might be asking what my qualifications are to be writing a book about gender, and my answer is predominantly lived experience. I was assigned female at birth (AFAB), and I didn't think there was anything exceptionally wrong with that until I started college in  the fall of 2019. You'll hear that story in theatrical detail in Chapter 3, so we can skip ahead for the moment. After a gender identity crisis and a few tearful conversations, I concluded that I'm transmasculine nonbinary. In a nutshell, that means that the gender binary doesn't fit me well. I've legally and medically transitioned away from the "femaleness" assigned to me at birth and toward a presentation that is charmingly genderqueer in how I define it. I've come out, legally changed my name, started hormone replacement therapy (HRT), undergone top surgery, and passed through many iterations of pronouns. If your eyes are glazing over, don't worry—I'll explain all these terms in the next chapter, I promise! And at present, I use two sets of pronouns: they/them/theirs and he/him/his.

All this to say, I've steadily and profoundly interacted with gender for years, and I enjoy comparing my notes with others, no matter where they're at in their conceptions of gender. I want non-cis and cis people alike to have more safe spaces to analyze and confront what they've been taught to believe about gender, and I want to increase the accessibility of these conversations. I've talked about gender with every person I'm close to at least once in the last month, if not in the last *week*. We're all watching as gender exploration and gender variance gain some visibility and respect, but these discussions aren't spreading at the rate they need to be, so you've got me here as your gender friend to help get the ball rolling.

I won't claim to have every answer or perspective on gender—no one does. As a thin, currently able-bodied, college-educated, lighter-skinned, lower-to-middle class, "passing" and "conventionally attractive," transmasculine nonbinary person, I know that my experiences with gender aren't universal by any means. My goal is simply to supply you with stories and suggestions that'll give you a home base to work from as you start changing your gendered relationships with yourself, your family, your friends, your co-workers, your gym buddies, your congregations, and all the other people you encounter for the better.

Lastly, as we set out on this path, I want to encourage you to reach out if you'd like to share your story with me at any stage of your gender journey. You'll always be able to find me at *orphoenixtheauthor@gmail.com*. I'd love to hear from you.

CHAPTER 2

What Words Should
We Be Using?

When you think of the queer community, you'll likely picture the phrase "LGBTQ+"; you may know a lengthier or shortened version of that acronym, but that is where most of our knowledge is commonly built from. The fullest acronym I've heard is "LGBTQ2SIADP+." The plus (+) is still present in that rendition, which is striking to me. A 12-character term still doesn't capture a fully accurate picture of our community. There are nuances that are difficult to define and even more difficult to cram into an acronym that is already elongated beyond what some consider "acceptable."

In case your eyes started to glaze over when I began to recount my gender earlier, I want to dedicate a brief chapter to providing you with definitions. I don't want to assume you've spent any time in Gender and Sexuality 101 courses or trainings, and even if you have, you may have forgotten some key terms in the time since. As you read this text, you'll be able to refer back to this chapter as needed when a term trips you up. Think of this as your surprise glossary. And if you're reading this in the semi-distant future, and you've got words or definitions to add, I'll leave space at the end for you to toss those in!

Disclaimer: These are my definitions. They're informed by many readings and conversations, but they're still imperfect and non-exhaustive. They're different from ten years ago, and they're different from ten years from now. My definitions also center on transmasculinity—if you're in search of trans*feminine* key terms and explanations, I'd recommend finding transfemme writers/artists/activists/speakers/YouTubers/ TikTokers that you can learn from. I don't want to speak for them. Please take these limitations into account as you read.

AGENDER: Genderless, gender neutral.

ANDROGYNOUS: Encompasses forms of masculinity and femininity.

ASSIGNED FEMALE AT BIRTH (AFAB): Designates a person assigned female from a person assigned male or intersex.

ASSIGNED MALE AT BIRTH (AMAB): Designates a person assigned male from a person assigned female or intersex.

BINARY TRANS: Trans women and trans men.

BINDING: Flattening the appearance of an individual's breasts through a chest binder, wrap, or tight piece of clothing.

For reference, this is what my first binder looked like, in summer 2020.

CISGENDER, CIS: When an individual's gender matches their assigned sex.

CISHET: An abbreviation for "cisgender heterosexual."

CISNORMATIVITY: Assuming everyone you encounter is cisgender.

CLOSETED: Not openly disclosing one's identity; commonly used in reference to gender or sexuality.

COMING OUT: Beginning to openly identify with and/or share one's identity with others; commonly used in reference to gender or sexuality.

DEADNAME: Birth name of an individual who has since changed their name.

DE-TRANSITION: Pausing one's transition and/or returning to a gender identity more closely associated with the sex one was assigned at birth.

ENBYPHOBIA: Unjustified fear of and/or prejudice against nonbinary individuals.

ENDOCRINOLOGIST: A medical professional who works with hormones.

FEMALE: An individual who identifies as female.

FEMME: Feminine.

FEMALE TO MALE (FTM): Transitioning from identifying as female to identifying as male.

FEMALE TO NONBINARY (FTN/FTX): Transitioning from identifying with a female cis gender to identifying as nonbinary.

GENDER: How an individual understands their gender.

GENDER AFFIRMING: Contributing a positive and more comfortable association with one's most authentic understanding of their gender.

GENDER ATTRIBUTION: The use of audio and visual cues in an attempt to infer how others "should" be gendered.

GENDER BINARY: Faulty suggestion of two and only two genders that sit on opposite sides of the binary.

GENDER DYSPHORIA: Negative, personal reactions to a nonalignment of one's assigned sex and gender.

GENDER EUPHORIA: Positive, personal reactions to one's gender being recognized and respected.

GENDER EXPRESSION/PRES-ENTATION: How an individual communicates their gender.

For my stage makeup course in the fall of 2021, I was given the chance to create a makeup look based on Prince, and it was an affirming and exhilarating experience.

GENDER JOURNEY: How one's relationship to and understanding of their gender changes, develops, and/or deepens over time.

GENDER LITERACY: The ability to discuss gender with inclusion and respect at the forefront.

GENDER NEUTRAL/NON-CONFORMING: Operating outside or away from the gender binary.

GENDERQUEER: Expressing gender non-normatively.

GETTING "CLOCKED": When a non-cisgender individual is recognized as not being cisgender.

GOING STEALTH: Living life without letting others know of any personal non-cisgender lived experience.

HORMONE REPLACEMENT THERAPY (HRT): Taking hormones to alter one's presentation.

LGBTQ2SIADP+: Lesbian, gay, bisexual, transgender, trans, queer, questioning, two spirit, intersex, asexual, demisexual, pansexual, and all marginalized genders and sexualities not listed.

MASC: Masculine.

MALE: An individual who identifies as male.

MALE TO FEMALE (MTF): Transitioning from identifying as male to identifying as female.

MALE TO NONBINARY (MTN/MTX): Transitioning from identifying with a male cis gender to identifying as nonbinary.

MAN: An individual who identifies as a man.

MISGENDER: Assigning an individual the wrong pronoun/s and/or gendered terms, either by accident or with malicious intent.

MISNAMING: Using the wrong name for an individual, either by accident or with malicious intent.

NEOPRONOUNS: Any pronouns that aren't she/her/hers, he/him/his, or they/them/theirs.

NONBINARY, ENBY: An individual who identifies as non-binary, not falling within the gender binary.

PASSING, PASSING PRIVILEGE: Being perceived correctly, or as desired, by others.

I frequently aim to pass as a cis man when I'm traveling alone, for my safety. This is what I typically look like when I'm going for a run or to the on-campus gym.

PRONOUNS: Words used to refer to an individual in place of their name.

TESTOSTERONE, T: Hormone commonly used in HRT to alter one's presentation, typically taken by persons assigned female at birth.

TGNCNB: Trans, gender non-conforming, and/or nonbinary.

TOP SURGERY (FTN/FTX/FTM VERSION): Removal of excess, unwanted breast tissue.

TRANSFEMININE: Refers to individuals who are assigned male at birth and are shifting away from that label.

TRANSGENDER, TRANS: Refers to an individual whose gender differs from their assigned sex; who identifies as transgender or trans.

TRANSITIONING: Beginning to live as an individual's true gender, however that manifests for them.

TRANSITION PRIVILEGE: Having access to the resources needed to transition as an individual would like.

TRANSMASCULINE: Refers to individuals who were assigned female at birth and are shifting away from that label.

TRANS NONBINARY, NONBINARY TRANS: Refers to individuals who identify as both transgender and nonbinary.

TRANSPHOBIA: Unjustified fear of and/or prejudice against trans individuals.

WOMAN: An individual who identifies as a woman.

. . . .

. . . .

. . . .

. . . .

. . . .

CHAPTER 3

How Did I Become Oakley?

I wasn't born Oakley. In fact, I didn't become Oakley until the end of 2019. I want to share my coming out (as nonbinary) story with you because it helps to ground us, and it zeroes in on the specifics of what we're getting at: intimately connecting you with a genderqueer person. As your gender friend, I want our connection to be personal and authentic. So, if you'll allow me, I'm going to transport you back to the fall of 2019. *All of the names you're going to read, including my deadname, have been changed to protect confidentiality. This is a dramatized version of the story, but all events are true.*

* * *

Jordan couldn't stomach anything more than her oatmeal. She sat facing her moms at the restaurant's faded table and bit at the insides of her cheeks. In theory, Jordan was ready for her first day of college at Willamette; she'd made checklist after checklist and Pinterest board after Pinterest board, but, in practice, she was a nervous wreck.

Her time at St. Basil St. Crispin, or "SBSC" for short, had been harsher than she'd allowed herself to realize. Jordan blended in as best she could, packing her calendar with sports and student leadership roles to distract from her presence on campus as the queer daughter of two lesbian women. The daughter "born of sin," as her health ethics teacher had phrased it. Jordan expected Willamette to be better. It was in northern Oregon, first of all, which was different from the Bay Area—it was green, and it didn't look as if everything had recently been on fire.

Jordan left her moms in her dorm room to decide how best to set up her bed and walked alone to Willamette's orientation: New Beginnings.

"My name is Tenley, I'm a sophomore, and I use she/her pronouns." Jordan's New Beginnings leader smiled and encouraged the student to her left to introduce themself next. Jordan blinked and looked around, hoping someone else appeared as lost as she felt. *She/her pronouns? Am I supposed to know what that means?*

Jordan made an educated guess when it was her turn, "Hi, I'm Jordan, but most people call me J. I use she/her pronouns." Everywhere she went, pronouns followed. Pronouns of all sorts. She/her. He/him. They/them. It was a new world, far from the gendered rules and regulations of SBSC where something as simple as having a non-naturally occurring hair color was forbidden. When Jordan went to audition for Willamette's hip-hop dance club, Deviate, she learned that the club's captain used she/they pronouns. *You can mix and match?*

* * *

"There's a possibility I will start using she/they pronouns and like it. I didn't know what pronouns *were* before I started at Willamette. I wanna understand why some people prefer to be addressed like this," Cannon nodded politely as Jordan rambled through half-formed thoughts in her dorm room one sunny fall afternoon.

"Here...I've been wanting to try she/they pronouns too. We can do it together, J. That'll make things easier," and the two were off to the races from there. Jordan was right; she did enjoy the ambiguity of she/they pronouns, the un-gendering of it and the freedom that that came with. Jordan laughed when she pictured the shock and horror on her health ethics teacher's face if she ever found out.

* * *

Jordan fidgeted as they spaced out in their afternoon class on feminism, gender, and society. It wasn't because they didn't enjoy the class; they simply had other things on their mind. As Jordan stole glances at her classmates, she counted the number of people who openly used they/them pronouns exclusively—3 out of 15. Jordan was quietly intimidated by every person in that classroom, but those three people specifically held her attention. *What gave them the confidence to only use they/them? Didn't they have family members and friends who didn't understand them? How were they brave enough to do it anyway?*

* * *

Jordan laid sprawled across Cannon's dark green comforter and stared at the plastic spiders stuck to the wall, "What's the worst that could happen if I only use they/them? My moms wouldn't disown me. They're not allowed to. They're *lesbians.* That would be false advertising to be transphobic lesbians, right?" Cannon laughed and agreed to shift to only using they/them pronouns for Jordan as long as they did the same for Cannon.

* * *

This is a trap. Building a just society from scratch is not something you should ask college first years to do. Jordan paced the campus library, thinking thoughts at double-time. They were overthinking their first college final project, and they knew it. For Willamette's intro-to-college seminar course titled "What is a Just Society?" Jordan was expected to design an equitable society from scratch using what they'd learned in class. Jordan flopped down onto the couch where they'd been sitting and typed into the search bar: *nonbinary names.*

The only element of their project they were certain of was that the leaders of their society would be nonbinary or gender non-conforming. The search came back with hundreds of names: Honor, Mari, Sky, Bailey, Oakley.

...*Oakley.* Jordan set their laptop aside and let their head rest in their hand as they watched the orange leaves fall. *Hi, I'm Oakley. I love your earrings! Would you want to grab coffee sometime?* It was too perfect, too easy, too obvious. Jordan felt the warmth of the name wash over them. They'd subconsciously considered changing their name before, and reading the name "Oakley" on their computer screen had sealed the deal. They'd always hated their last name, and they'd grown more distant from their legal first name as they'd begun exploring their gender this semester. *Was this the next step on a path Jordan simply couldn't make a checklist for?*

* * *

"Okay, picture this, Cannon! Hi, I'm Oakley, and I'll be your Willamette tour guide for today," Jordan read over the notes on their application to become an Admission Ambassador for the university.

Cannon smiled, "It fits well." Jordan twirled around Cannon's dorm room in the goofy, oddly-reminiscent-of-getting-ready-for-prom sort of way.

* * *

Why aren't they more excited? How can two interracial lesbians not be accepting of their genderqueer kid? That is indeed false advertising. Jordan looked down at the floor as they ended the call with their moms. They'd been perfectly eloquent and to the point, "I'm thinking of changing my name. I'm in college now, and I'm figuring out who I am. I'm not completely sure yet, but I'm considering the name Oakley, Oak for short." Leslie didn't seem to think much of the idea, but Gina *hated* it. Jordan wanted their moms to be fully supportive of their decision, and that wasn't the case. Jordan crawled into bed and watched some dance videos on YouTube before falling asleep with a resolution to turn back to the drawing board, placing all of their genderqueer plans on hold.

* * *

Jordan still hadn't figured out how to make their gender more palatable to their parents, and it had been weeks. She'd backtracked, returning to only using she/her pronouns and asking Cannon to stop calling her Oakley because it was overwhelming. She'd been wandering without a plan for her evening when she found a few of her friends answering "The 36 Questions That Lead to Love" in the basement of one of Willamette's academic buildings. Jordan decided to join Cannon, Garrett, and Melodie for the final handful of questions.

Melodie read the next question aloud as dramatically as you'd expect a theatre kid to, "If you knew that in one year you would die suddenly, would you change anything about the way you are now living? Why?" Jordan listened patiently as each person answered. There was an awkward silence as she thought of her response. She eventually blurted out, "I'd want everyone to know me as Oakley."

Garrett laughed, and Jordan took slight offense, "What?"

He nodded and grinned, "You know, if you care enough about this that it's the one thing you would do differently if you knew you were gonna *die* in a year, you might want to take it seriously. Especially considering you aren't actually dying." Garrett had a point, and Jordan knew it.

* * *

Jordan was busy putting the finishing touches on their final projects for the fall. They were proud of their beautifully queer and just society, powerfully vulnerable zine that ended with "A Letter to Oakley," and their other thorough and well-researched final papers. In between editing slideshows and proofreading essays, Jordan turned to genderqueer YouTube videos, journal entries, and lengthy checklists. As lovably task-oriented as Jordan was, they'd managed to find a way to systematize their plans for coming out as nonbinary and starting to transition:

Step 1: Tell my Willamette friends that I want to be called Oakley (or Oak for short).

Step 2: Start using the all-gender restrooms on campus.

Step 3: Get my Willamette student ID card changed to my new name.

Step 4: Come out to my moms and other non-Willamette loved ones.

Step 5: Start T.

Step 6: Get top surgery.

Little by little, Oakley started checking off the boxes and taking steps to affirm their new identity. Then, they were forced to leave campus...for winter break.

* * *

The McDonald's in Oakley's hometown was a cruddy place to work, even before they'd come out as nonbinary. Grouchy old white men in the mornings who hadn't had their coffee yet either flirted with Oakley or made their morning miserable in other ways. Oakley had elected *not* to come out to their 50+ co-workers, so they weren't Oakley (they/them) by day; they were Jordan (she/her) instead, and it was exhausting. Every time "Jordan" would get off work, they'd yank off their McDonald's nametag and sigh as though they were breathing out toxic air.

Thankfully, Oakley was fully out to their moms, though that wasn't going particularly well either. Their name could've been "Jord-Oakley" because that was all their moms consistently called them. They weren't yet seen as Oakley, and they weren't seen as nonbinary either. They were seen as Jordan, the girl who didn't want to be a girl anymore.

Oakley spent that winter break making frappes and ice cream cones and answering odd, invasive questions about their gender for other people—questions *they* barely had the answers to.

"Why would you change your name if it's already gender neutral?"

"What should people call you if you aren't a woman or a young lady anymore?"

"Do you think you'll medically transition in any way?"

In spite of the seemingly dreadful winter break in California, it wasn't all bad. Oakley ended up going to the court with Gina in January of 2020 to have their name legally changed, and the State approved it in April. Oakley reveled in that win even as the mountain of other forms of identification that needed updates piled high. Their state ID, passport, Social Security, birth certificate, credit cards, health insurance, email addresses, and Spotify account—just to name a few. But, with their name change taken care of, Oakley felt a new sense of agency and urgency and began to plow ahead toward starting testosterone and getting top surgery, the final two items on their old checklist.

* * *

And that's where we'll stop. I'll give you a moment to readjust to the present day...

Hi. Hello there. Welcome back! Now you know how I became Oakley, in 2000 words or less. Thank you for taking the time to read through my coming out story and learn how my own gender journey began. Let's take some time to reflect before moving on. There's room for you to answer the questions right on the page, so please do so!

EXERCISE 1

What led Oakley to come out as nonbinary?

. . . .

. . . .

. . . .

What seemed to be the hardest part of coming out for Oakley?

. . . .

. . . .

. . . .

Who supported Oakley in their coming out process?

. . . .

. . . .

. . . .

How did Oakley make sense of and organize their
gender journey?

. . . .

. . . .

. . . .

CHAPTER 4

Let's Start Thinking About Your Gender!

Let's catch our breath. Breathe in, breathe out. Go grab a glass of water. Stretch for a few moments. Re-ground yourself. That was a considerable amount of time spent talking at you, so let's re-focus on you and *your* story! Now that you know what led me to explore my gender and how I began my coming out process, I want you to embark on a similar self-reflection period. I don't expect you to make any life-altering decisions after answering the coming questions, but I *do* want you to begin to think about your gender more critically than (potentially) ever before. You're welcome to utilize the space left on the page to write down your answers, and it may come in handy later on to be able to easily look back at what you've written!

EXERCISE 2

How would you define or describe your gender to another person? Are there any words, phrases, images, people, or characters that would be helpful in providing that explanation?

. . . .

. . . .

. . . .

Have you interacted with any individual/s whose gender/s seem unique or different from what you're accustomed to? If yes, which aspects of their gender identity or expression were most striking to you?

. . . .

. . . .

. . . .

Do you ever feel restricted by your gender presentation? Safety, freedom, performance, profession, and interpersonal connections are common themes that may bubble up to the surface here. If you answered yes to this question, could you elaborate?

. . . .

. . . .

. . . .

If you were able to pick an item to incorporate into your life from a gender presentation that is considered "off-limits" for you, what would you pick and why? Think leggings, boxers, dresses, makeup, haircuts, hair lengths, nail polish, and so on. What is holding you back from this item?

. . . .

. . . .

. . . .

Thank you for taking the time to sit with these questions. I'd encourage you to share your responses with any individuals you feel comfortable opening up to; you're welcome to ask for their answers too! Spending dedicated time unpacking what we think we know about gender is vital to being able to move past the limits and lectures we've internalized throughout our lives thus far. Remember that the rules we have in place in relation to gender are profoundly arbitrary, and they change based on when and where you're looking.

Regardless of how straightforward or arduous this exercise was for you, you did it, and that's magnificent. You have plenty of time to sit with what you wrote and process it, and I'll be here to help you along the way!

CHAPTER 5

So, What's Your Gender, Oakley?

[We sit down at your favorite local coffee shop after I order you your preferred beverage and a blended chai for myself.]

YOU: It's nice to meet you. I'm [NAME]. I'd like to learn more about your gender, if that would be alright. I'm hoping to meet more people who aren't cisgender so that I can understand more and be able to become a better advocate.

OAKLEY: I'd be happy to share more information with you, and I'm glad you took the time to reach out! Coffee and conversations like these are how I spend most of my weekends these days.

[You take a sip of your drink and open your notebook, choosing which question to ask first.]

YOU: We can start simple. Could you describe your gender to me, first, as if I knew next to nothing about gender and then, second, as if I were one of your most trusted allies in gender advocacy?

[I smile at you.]

OAKLEY: I haven't been asked that before. First, I'd say something to the effect of, "My gender is a little all over the place. I don't categorize myself as a man or a woman exclusively, because I know that my experience has been more complicated than that... I've come to view my gender as a potluck, a collaborative effort between me and the people who inspire me. Picture a potluck where recipes have been passed down and people are experimenting with new flavor combinations. I do something similar with my gender. It's based on taking what I learned growing up and remixing that as I see new gender expressions that catch my attention and excite me." At the end of the day, I'm not able to be boxed into a binary understanding of gender, so I usually call myself nonbinary and leave it at that unless I'm asked to give more detail.

[You stare at me wide-eyed and take a breath.]

YOU: Wait...that's what you'd say to me if I didn't understand gender? That was extensive!

[I turn a bit red and laugh.]

OAKLEY: I—whoops—I forgot to water down my answer... I don't know that I describe my gender all that differently depending on who I'm talking to. The main change is how much time I spend providing context and breaking down more obscure terminology.

YOU: That's understandable. My next question...you described your gender as a "collaborative effort." How does that manifest in your day-to-day life?

[I take out my phone to show a few pictures.]

This is me with my family right after graduating high school in the spring of 2019. Look at all that hair!

OAKLEY: Before coming out as nonbinary, I had no understanding of how I could buck gender norms to enjoy expressing myself more. High school was a different time. I was on senior prom court for crying out loud! I just didn't spend any time questioning the boxes I'd been placed in until I started college. These pictures encapsulate who I was before college, and I'm happy to no longer be that person. Where the collaborative aspect that you mentioned before comes in, is checking in with my loved ones and learning more about how they're conceptualizing their genders these days, then remembering what I can from those conversations and implementing the pieces I'd most like to try. Sometimes it's as simple as asking if I can borrow my partner's sweater that's been bringing them gender euphoria, or it's as complex as unpacking what makes my friend a cis man. It's a sustained, shifting discussion with many moving parts.

YOU: Interesting! So, how would you describe your personal style? That seems pretty connected to how you understand your gender.

OAKLEY: You're right about that. My aesthetic color-wise is largely based in earth tones and neutrals, and fit-wise, it's either cozy and oversized or fairly form-fitting. Picture a cross between Corbin Bleu in *High School Musical*, Chidi Anagonye from *The Good Place*, David Rose from *Schitt's Creek*, and Park Jimin and Kim Taehyung from BTS.

[I show several pictures of attractive men that do seem to add up to roughly what I look like.]

OAKLEY: You also picked up on how externalized my gender is. My gender and my outfits go hand in hand, which isn't a universal experience by any means. I'd like for my gender expression to inspire others and invite them to experiment. I'd love for an individual to see me and think, "I'd like to try wearing something like that!" I'd love to see more people playing with gender and highlighting how irrational our rules are. My hope would be that, eventually, every person presents themselves in a way that makes them feel like they're the coolest person on Earth. For me, that typically manifests in dressing like a nerdy college kid in a coffee shop one day, a twink in a gay bar the next, and a queer college professor the day after that.

YOU: I love that for you! What, if anything, would you consider borrowing from my gender expression? What could I add to the potluck that is Oakley's gender?

OAKLEY: I'd leave that up to you! If you have a necklace or a sweater that you particularly enjoy, I might take that for a spin and return it to you later.

YOU: Next question, how have you been privileged throughout your gender journey?

OAKLEY: That's an excellent question. I have legally, socially, and medically transitioned in the ways I'd hoped for. Becoming Oakley freed me from my old name, which felt very directly tied to me being perceived as a young woman. Starting T gave me access to a list of physical attributes that allow me to feel more at home in my body. And having top surgery unlocked a number of big and little things that I simply couldn't do or couldn't *feel safe* doing before. Living in the Pacific Northwest, having access to a healthcare plan that provided funds for gender-affirming care, and having a mom who wanted to learn how to support me were all crucial in shaping my gender journey thus far, and each of those were enormous privileges.

[You finish up your drink and adjust how you're seated.]

YOU: Next question, and this is a heavy one: as a Black trans person, how does keeping yourself safe play into everything you've shared with me today?

[I take a moment to gather my thoughts.]

OAKLEY: There are two questions that cross my mind every day when I'm getting ready: (1) where am I going today, and (2) will I be safe wearing this outfit there? It's depressing, and it shouldn't be the case, but it's necessary as a Black trans genderqueer person living in the States today. I'm always going to be unsafe, but I can do little things to help mitigate that danger. In short, I dress and act differently if I know that I'll be spending all day at home or on campus, versus if I'm getting groceries and then walking past the Oregon State Capitol to spend some time alone downtown.

YOU: That makes sense. Final question, as I'd like to wrap this up on a lighter note: what questions would you recommend every person asks themselves when they're beginning to figure out their gender expression?

OAKLEY: Of course! I'd start simple: ask yourself what you'd like to wear, what accessories and makeup interest you, what you'd like your vibes to be, and what you want your presentation to say about you.

YOU: Thank you for your time, Oakley! I'm glad we got to sit down and chat. And thanks for the drink too!

CHAPTER 6

How Do I Create My Gender Euphoria?

When you think of gender, is your first thought "gender euphoria?" No, didn't think so. It's easy to lose sight of; when we're focused on getting through the day without a mass of gender *dys*phoria or on ignoring the nuances of gender completely, the concept of gender euphoria can get lost in all the hustle and bustle.

If the term itself is a bit tricky to understand, I have a simple analogy for you. Picture a department store dressing room. You're trying on a new shirt, and you walk out of the dressing room to get your friend's opinion. They take one look at you and give you a huge thumbs up. That thumbs up is how gender euphoria feels! When you feel affirmed and respected in your gender, when you know that you're moving with some swag in your step, when you finally see yourself reflected in your name and pronouns, when you catch a glimpse of yourself in the mirror and think, "Damn, look at you!"—those are the moments I'm referring to.

If you're cis, or beginning to question your cisness, you may not have realized that you've already had moments of gender euphoria, but I'm sure you have, even if they've been few and far between. To be clear, gender euphoria isn't exclusive to trans people or cis people or any other gender grouping. Everyone can access it if they're given the space and support to do a bit of exploring and experimenting.

To help you along in this exploration, I've compiled a list of the ways in which I find my own gender euphoria. If you see something you like, try it out! Without further ado...

Oakley, where does gender euphoria come from?

1. **Not boxing myself in.** Transmasculinity can sometimes feel like another box I'm expected to fit into, but worrying about whether or not I'm doing masculinity, or *trans*masculinity is, well, more stress than it's worth. I'd rather present how I'd like to on any given day than hold myself back out of fear of potentially making some arbitrary misstep.

2. **Seeking inspiration.** The number of Pinterest

boards I made during the summer of 2020 when I was deciding what I wanted my aesthetic to be, after having spent years ruining my sense of style (read: wearing uniforms at SBSC HS), was absurd...but it worked. I learned how to accessorize for different looks, the power of layering, and how to style color-complementary outfits as opposed to color-coordinated outfits. Nowadays, I go to thrift shops when I've saved up, and I find more exciting and outlandish pieces to add to my wardrobe.

3. **Being kind to myself.** I haven't felt much gender dysphoria lately, and I'm grateful for that. I remember how I used to look at my chest and just feel...bad and wrong. There are still moments where I see my hips or how a shirt fits and get a little bummed because my body isn't necessarily doing what I'd like it to, but I try to move past those feelings and give myself the benefit of the doubt. My body is pretty rockin', and I aim to approach my dysphoric moments with that in mind.

4. **Standing up for myself.** I've been out long enough to have succinct soundbite responses to most inappropriate or inconsiderate remarks. I know that my gender is valid, and I know that I'm

not in the wrong for making sure that I'm being given respect. Something as simple as, "I go by Oakley now" or, "I don't like being referred to in that way" comes naturally, and it makes me feel better to stand my ground in uncomfortable gender-related situations.

5. **Finding and utilizing affirming spaces.** It's much easier to do gender with others who understand its complexities. There's a student-run club at my university called QTPOC (Queer Trans People of Color), and it's where I turn when I just need to be around people who get it. Willamette is a predominantly white institution, and with that comes predominantly white queer spaces, so having QTPOC as a safe space means the world for me on days where I'm exhausted by the sheer amount of work I do to keep myself safe.

6. **Making friends who only know me as Oakley.** I can't perfectly capture how much gender euphoria this gives me. I've finally reached a point at Willamette where the younger students don't know my old name, and it's incredible. In their eyes, I've only ever been Oakley, and that's validating in such a specific way—like they've only ever known the most authentic version of me. I'm really proud of my name and what it

represents, and having folks in my social circles who simply call me Oakley without ever having known different is the best.

7. **Watching loved ones create their own gender euphoria.** As I mentioned earlier, I'm something of an unofficial gender therapist for a lot of people in my life, and I'm always thrilled to see my friends and family make changes and grow in ways that affirm them. Hearing about name changes, watching someone's style evolve, listening to a friend describe how they've come to conceptualize their gender, all of these hit the spot euphoria-wise. I love seeing other folks grapple with gender and come out the other side more connected to themselves.

8. **Learning about genders different from my own.** There's a section later in this text full of recommended non-cis artists to support, and those people are my digital go-tos for learning and being challenged. I never want to pretend that I've got all the gender answers because that wouldn't be fair to anyone, and it would also be absolutely exhausting. Listening to other people's lived experiences with gender and seeing the intersections of our stories along with where they splinter off can be really eye-opening for

me because I've only experienced one specific set of identities that complicate my gender journey. In short, knowledge is power, folks.

9. **Knowing that I know myself best.** This may seem obvious, but it can be hard to remember sometimes. When I sit down to journal or simply to mindlessly crochet while processing my other thoughts, I really get to connect with myself and understand how I operate more deeply. When it comes to my gender, I know what I need in order to feel good, and I also know what won't work for me. There's a massive misconception that there are gender specialists somewhere pulling all the strings and convincing people to "come to the dark side" and take hormones or have surgery, but that *really* isn't the case. We know what's going to spark our own gender euphoria and what, on the other hand, will stamp it out.

10. **Letting time take time.** I know that my gender journey isn't finished, and I'm okay with that. If I woke up one morning and suddenly felt and looked exactly like the person I want to be, I don't think I'd be excited for more than a few hours. I like the process of growing and challenging what I think I know. I'm glad that I'm starting the work of unpacking and understanding my

gender now so that I can enjoy the rewards of that labor sooner.

Searching for the 'thumbs-up' moments is its own mini-journey, but I hope that my two cents on finding gender joy can help you along in your search!

CHAPTER 7

Ignorance Ain't Bliss— It's Time for a Question Break!

N ow I'm guessing you've still got a lot of questions, even after our impromptu coffee date. As I've spent more time out of the closet, I've grown more comfortable answering questions that could be considered private, personal, or invasive. Over the past few years, I've learned how to separate my current self from my past self when describing aspects of my transition (my old name, my pre-op chest, etc.) to avoid triggering any sour emotions for me. To be clear, not all non-cis people are interested in opening up to you, and we don't owe anyone any explanations. I happen to like talking about all of this, and I'm glad to provide some first-hand perspective so that individuals who haven't encountered these lived experiences have more access to information that can help them become better advocates and allies.

Okay, let's get started! Grab some tea (or some T!) and a comfy blanket, sit back, and enjoy the ride.

* * *

First question: why did I change my name, especially given that my birth name was already considered gender neutral?

I changed my name from Jordan to Oakley because I wanted a name that had never been associated with gendered language when it was used for me. When I was known as Jordan, I was also known as a daughter, a young woman, a little sister, and a girlfriend. Oak/Oakley provided a fresh start for me, without any personal womanly baggage.

Next question: why did I medically transition?

I wanted to take control over my body and how it was perceived. I needed to feel freer to express myself and my gender in a variety of ways that weren't accessible for me without having top surgery and starting T.

35 perks of being post-op top surgery

1. Not needing to wear a binder to feel safe enough or confident enough to leave my room.

2. No longer hurting my chest from binding.

3. Not getting misgendered because of my chest.

4. Feeling that dysphoria is alleviated.

5. Being able to comfortably reclaim my femininity.

6. Breathing more easily.

7. Getting to give physical affection to others without worrying about whether or not they could feel my pre-op chest.

8. Not having to think about my chest all the time.

9. Being able to pass with more ease, when I want to.

10. No longer having to hunch over, awkwardly carry my shirt out in front of me, or cross my arms over my chest to hide when I'm not wearing a binder.

11. Not having to plan my days around binding.

12. Not having to worry about my binder being visible underneath my clothes.

13. Not having to fight with my healthcare provider anymore.

14. Standing up straight, and with confidence.

You can see from my graduation picture that my chest was never particularly large, but becoming surgically flat-chested in October 2020 was still right for me, in spite of the concerns raised by others.

15. Showering in peace.

16. Going swimming in peace.

17. Dancing in peace.

18. Getting to show off my top surgery scars.

19. Getting to be shirtless in public without it being illegal.

20. Sleeping shirtless comfortably.

21. Being able to change around others without feeling shame, fear, or discomfort.

22. Not owning a single bra.

23. Getting to put my towel around my waist after I shower, instead of around my midsection.

24. Getting to feel a shirt against my bare chest.

25. Getting to wear form-fitting tops and un-buttoned shirts without having to think about my chest.

26. Working out comfortably.

27. Taking shirtless selfies.

28. Having pecs.

29. Not overheating because of my binder.

30. Proving to myself that top surgery exists beyond the internet.

31. Proving to doubtful family members and friends that top surgery was the right decision for me.

32. Being a visibly trans person on my college campus and showing others that it's okay.

33. Smiling when I catch a glimpse of myself in the mirror.

34. Taking control of my body.

35. Feeling at home in my body.

Next, how has T impacted me?

I'd like to preface this by saying that hormones affect every individual differently. HRT is *not* a uniform experience by any means, and I can't emphasize that strongly enough. In other words, your mileage may vary (YMMV). For me personally, I can breakdown the changes I've experienced from T into a relatively simple list.

Pros:

- *Body fat redistribution*—broader shoulders, more "Dorito shaped"

This is me in the fall of 2019, pre-T, sporting a comfortable ex-swimmer's physique and some facial "baby fat."

- *Increased ability to grow muscle* (assisted by having a workout routine)
- *Facial fat redistribution*—sharper jawline, less "baby faced"

This is me in the fall of 2021. You can see how my face has slimmed and how my upper body has become more defined.

- *Lower voice*—went from an alto to a bass-leaning baritone
- *Increased facial hair*—incoming mustache, hints of a beard
- *Stopped menstruating*—cycle stopped at four months on T
- *Bottom growth*—altered how I experience intimacy in significant, affirming ways
- *Increased libido*—changed how frequently I interact with my sexual partner(s)
- *Different smell*—muskier scent now.

Cons:

- *Increased acne*—had to go on a six-month round of Accutane to get a handle on my persistent mild acne
- *Difficulty crying*—can't cry unless I'm deeply moved, as opposed to crying whenever I'd like
- *Receded hairline*—thinning hair near my temples
- *Second puberty*—nobody wants that.

In sum, I'm glad to have gone on T. I'm grateful for the relative freedom and safety the changes from T have given me. If you're considering starting HRT or you're in the earlier stages of it, you've got this. You'll see plenty of changes that you love, and you can always pause, adjust your dosage, change your injection site or method, or otherwise re-evaluate as needed if you encounter changes you aren't a fan of.

In line with questions related to top surgery and T, I'm often asked: do I want to pass?

First, I take issue with the concept of passing. Passing implies that (1) each person must abide by the rules of their gender's most commonly understood presentation in order to be respected within their gender identity, and (2) each non-cis person can't truly be the gender they're "passing" as. Put simply, the concept of passing upholds the gender binary by attempting to decide what each person's gender can look like and who's a believable member of each gender. When I say the words *nonbinary, woman,* and *man,* you'll likely picture something specific for each, and that's a bit of an issue. The three most commonly discussed genders shouldn't have locked-in descriptions. Anyone can be any gender, regardless of how they present.

The stereotypes for men and women have been shown to all of us excessively, but the stereotypes for nonbinary individuals are still up and coming. If I had to break the new stereotypes down into a single word, I'd say *androgyny.* If I had to offer you socially accepted "nonbinary physical attributes," I'd say thinness, a flat chest, vague masculinity, whiteness or proximity to whiteness, a lack of curves, and being assigned female at birth. That's a *lot* of boxes, and very few people can check them all off. Trying to pass as nonbinary, given these restrictions, is nearly impossible, and because of these newer rules, plenty of TGNCNB folks are automatically disqualified from being seen and respected as their authentic genders.

Even though I'm nonbinary, I don't necessarily try to—or even want to—pass as nonbinary all the time. Sometimes I need to pass as a cis man to keep myself safe (for example, in public restrooms or when I'm traveling alone). But, I'd like to be seen as nonbinary *most* of the time. Having medically and socially transitioned has helped substantially with my ability to "pass" as nonbinary, but those are privileges that plenty of people just don't have access to or have any interest in. Transitioning and "passing" shouldn't be prerequisites for being respected as the gender you'd like to be understood as. Every gender should be more accessible than that.

All non-cis people (and cis people as well) deserve to have the correct genders attributed to them without having to put any extra effort in. It should be that simple. If you're not cis, I promise your gender is valid no matter how you express it. If you *are* cis, I'd advise you to be more aware of how you're addressing your non-cis loved ones and how you're trying to show your support for them. When you're complimenting your loved ones, be mindful of what you're saying. You don't need to comment on how womanly, manly, or nonbinary they look. You can always just say that we look good or what it is exactly that you like about how we're presenting on any given day. Your comment doesn't need to relate to passing at all because the mere concept of passing is a *hot mess*, and it should probably be phased out entirely.

In short, it's complicated and the vast majority of us are still assumed to either be men or women no matter what we do, myself included. I want to be seen as nonbinary, but I don't necessarily want to pass in order for that to happen.

Last question: how did I convince the people in my life to make the transition to my new name and pronouns?

Truthfully, I *didn't* convince everyone. Only the people who genuinely cared about me made the transition. The people who didn't care didn't try, and few of them remain in my life today—which is another privilege I'm very grateful for. In my experience, it quickly became less about convincing people to care, and more about making sure that the people who *were* willing to try and understand had the support and resources they needed to make the shift a little easier. I tried to answer questions and be as patient as I could so that the allies in my life wanted to continue learning how to be there for me. For the people who did put the effort in, they needed little to no convincing. They knew that shifting to using my new name and pronouns was the only proper response, even if they needed lots of guidance to reach a point where they consistently addressed me correctly.

If you're shifting to a new name and/or pronouns, I hope you'll trust me when I say that there are people out there who will address you properly, and you deserve that. You deserve to be seen for who you really are, and I hope you are already surrounded by support or that you find that support soon. I'd highly encourage you to check out the Gender and Sexuality Alliances (GSAs) or other queer and trans support groups in your school, workplace, or region to find more people who are excited to be there for you throughout your gender journey.

If you're currently in the process of being "convinced" to use a loved one's proper name and pronouns, I'd advise you to hurry up and make that decision. I say this as lovingly as I can: your loved one needs you, and they need you to be on their team. Try as hard as you can not to make this about you. I'll provide more context, tips, and examples for the allies reading later in the book, but for now, I'd simply urge you to make the shift to your loved one's new name and/or pronouns as soon as you possibly can. You'll be glad you did.

CHAPTER 8

How Can I Support Myself Through a Gender Journey?

How are we doing? Do we want a stretch break? I'd recommend going for a brief stroll then coming back. We're about to dive into a heavier subject: supporting oneself through a gender journey. Now, what exactly does that mean? This chapter is geared toward questioning and confirmed non-cis individuals who are tackling gender on their own, for any reason. They may not be able to safely come out to the people in their lives, or they might not be sure where or how to start that process. Regardless of their/your exact circumstances, I'm here to help you feel less alone and make sure you've got some guidance as you begin navigating this work.

To the readers who don't currently have plans to embark on gender journeys but are here in search of tips and tricks should you ever happen to need them, I'm happy you're here too! This section will have value for people in all stages of their relationships to gender, I promise. No matter the reason you're reading, I'm glad you'll be joining me. I'll be introducing five suggestions for crafting your gender journey into a *path* you'd like to be on at a *pace* you're comfortable with. Let's get started!

Step 1: Create a list of who and/or what can support you through this process

EXERCISE 3

Who would you feel comfortable coming out to?

. . . .

. . . .

. . . .

Is there anyone you know who has transitioned (socially, legally, medically, etc.) who could serve as a resource for you?

. . . .

. . . .

. . . .

Are there any in-person or online support groups or gender-affirming resources you have access to?

. . . .

. . . .

. . . .

Our aim is to make sure you feel supported, however you'd like to be. When I began medically transitioning, I didn't have access to a strong, in-person support system. It was the beginning of summer 2020 when I started T, and that wasn't exactly the best time to be out frolicking through the fields with my closest trans and nonbinary friends...there was a pandemic starting. I began my blog *theoaknotes* in June 2020 because I needed an outlet to process what I was going through. I wanted to tell people what was happening, even if those people were members of the Internet Void. Somehow, that worked for me. I'd strongly recommend writing down your feelings about gender, even (and especially) if they don't end up on a blogging platform. It's nice to have a place to keep track of everything related to your gender journey and to eventually be able to look back and see how far you've come. At the end of the day, as long as you've got someone or something in your corner to provide you with some gender support, that'll help immensely.

Step 2: Envision how and what you'd like to change in relation to your gender, and create a gameplan or timeline

EXERCISE 4

How comfortable are you with how you currently dress?

. . . .

. . . .

. . . .

How do you feel about your name and pronouns?

. . . .

. . . .

. . . .

Do you like your voice? How about your hair (length, color, style, etc.)?

. . . .

. . . .

. . . .

How does the way you're gendered by others make you feel?

. . . .

. . . .

. . . .

What do you like most and least when you see yourself in a mirror?

. . . .

. . . .

. . . .

Start jotting down your thoughts. There are no wrong answers to these questions!

Trans Eye for the Supafly: Eight quick ways to find gender euphoria in your closet

You've heard of *Queer Eye for the Straight Guy* and its modern Netflix adaptation, right? If not, do a quick Google search and then head on back. I'd like to introduce you to *Trans Eye for the Supafly*, a quick detour to touch on gender and personal expression through fashion. You can (and should) go to local thrift shops, garage sales, and clothing swaps to make the following ideas more accessible and budget-friendly! You're also welcome to make Pinterest boards, lookbooks, zines, or journal entries based on these concepts instead of trying to make them all happen immediately, if that would be better for you.

1. Wear an article of clothing you've never worn before.

2. Try out a new accessory or makeup look.

3. Wear something incredibly *oversized*.

4. Wear something incredibly *form-fitting*.

5. Ask a loved one to make an outfit for you from *your* closet.

6. Ask a loved one to make an outfit for you from *their* closet.

7. Borrow or buy a pair of shoes that feel out of your league.

8. Dress up in a way you've never tried before.

These eight suggestions should get you started, but you're welcome to run with this concept! Get out of your comfort zone and figure out what's most affirming for you.

Lastly, if your body isn't conducive to this project yet, that's okay. I hear you. I know that some individuals won't try on a particular look or article of clothing because they know it won't look the way they want it to. You're always able to dip your toes into the gender-affirming water, even if it isn't the spectacular dive you dreamt it would be. Any gender euphoria beats no gender euphoria, right? Have fun, take care of yourself, and go get affirmed!

As you begin to zero in on thoughts and dreams for your gender, start prioritizing the changes according to what could happen when. What could happen immediately?

What would need to wait until you were in a safe/financially stable/comfortable/supported space? What could you accomplish given the confines of your home life, work life, and region? What could be covered by insurance or by your loved ones? What laws or other rules would you need to abide by within your country?

As you unpack these questions, understand that your gender journey's timeline is partly your choice and partly not, and it might not be an equal split. Hopefully, you'll be able to make many decisions and changes on the timing you'd prefer, but you may have to wait longer for some changes than you'd like. For example, I reached out to my healthcare provider about receiving top surgery in summer 2020, and they told me that it wasn't likely to happen before the spring of 2021. I was lucky enough to get surgery earlier than that due to another patient's cancellation, but that was a fluke. Waiting sucks, and I'm sorry in advance for any waiting you'll have to do. I hope this warning helps to prepare you, at least a little bit.

Break up your list of priorities into smaller projects that can be accomplished with the help of your support system, and delegate anything you can. See if your parent can help fill out paperwork, or ask your best friend to be your caretaker before and after a gender-affirming procedure. Look back at Step 1 to see who your allies are, and decide who can help you with what. You don't need to do this all on your own.

Step 3: Decide how (and if) your coming out process is going to occur

EXERCISE 5

Do you want to come out? If so, how?

. . . .

. . . .

. . . .

Who would you like to come out to?

. . . .

. . . .

. . . .

What information would you like to include when you're coming out to others?

. . . .

. . . .

. . . .

Who would react positively if you came out? Negatively? With indifference?

. . . .

. . . .

. . . .

I know it may seem unceremonious to write out the answers to questions as significant as these, but it's wise to think these things through before going into any coming out experience ill-prepped. It might not be in your self-esteem's best interest to come out to every relative you're certain will react negatively first. I'd recommend coming out to the allies first, to build up your safety net should a coming out go awry down the line. To give you an idea: if you know that your mom will be supportive when you come out to her but your grandma won't be, tell mom first. That way, she'll have your back when you tell grandma, and she'll be able to support you if you get hurt. Our goal with this step is to make sure no one's given enough power over your coming out experience to scare you back into the closet. This is your life, your story to tell, and you get to do it how you'd like to.

Step 4: Seek out and join safe and affirming spaces

EXERCISE 6

What LGBTQIA + resource centers, clubs, support groups, organizations, or committees are accessible to you?

. . . .

. . . .

. . . .

What affirming and educational films, talks, lectures, podcasts, workshops, or courses are being offered in person or digitally near you?

. . . .

. . . .

. . . .

I want you to find as many spaces as possible where you know you'll feel safe and supported in your gender journey. Use this page as a resource hub that you can circle back to as needed.

You don't need to frequent every place you've written down, but I want you to know that they're there if you need them. You aren't the first person to question your gender, and you won't be the last. There are loads of people out there who will see you and understand exactly what you're going through, and they'll be able to provide direct, personalized support for you.

I joined a virtual support group for transmasculine individuals during summer 2020, and it provided me with a safe space each week to ask questions I couldn't find the answers to anywhere else. *What's bottom growth? How long did it take for your voice to stop cracking? Where do you find trans elders? How long is the recovery for top surgery? Did anyone else need to start eating more after going on T? How did you pick your names?*

Random, wild questions that Google didn't know what to do with were calmly and thoughtfully answered in that space every Monday evening. It was a sanctuary where some things changed each week, but other things always stayed the same. I always looked forward to seeing whose voice deepened, who was comfortably recovering from top or bottom surgery, who'd just started T or changed their name or pronouns when I logged onto the call each week. Everything was always shifting, and it was incredible. I felt right at home, and I slowly grew into a person who could be relied on to help answer the questions I'd once asked.

I implore you to find a space (or several) where you're able to thrive as you make your way through this process. There are more gender friends out there, and you can find them if you just know where to look.

Gender-affirming recommendations to get you started

- **YouTubers:** Jackson Bird, Jammidodger, Angel and Nicole, madeyoulooks, MilesChronicles, Riley J. Dennis, Philosophy Tube, and Brendan Dunlap.

- **Books:** *The Deep* by Rivers Solomon, *Gender Outlaws: On Men, Women, and the Rest of Us* by Kate Bornstein, *Nonbinary: Memoirs of Gender and Identity* edited by Micah Rajunov and Scott Duane, *Some Assembly Required* by Arin Andrews, *Whipping Girl* by Julia Serano, *Stone Butch Blues* by Leslie Feinberg, *Sorted* by Jackson Bird, and *I Wish You All the Best* by Mason Deaver.

- **Podcasts and songs:** *Fruitbowl by Qubed Media, LLC, The Village by Wrabel, I/Me/Myself by Will Wood, and Explaining Jesus by Jordy Searcy.*

Step 5: Build your confidence

The final step of the "big five" when it comes to supporting yourself through a gender journey is gaining confidence in yourself. I know it's easy to try to gaslight ourselves into thinking (or listening to the voices of others that think) we're not valid or worthy of non-cisgender joy. You are valid, and you are worthy. No matter what. In spite of it all. Because of it all. Take another deep breath, and whisper it to yourself: *I'm valid, and I'm worthy.* Say it until you believe it.

You aren't expected to walk away from this section of the book with a precise, perfected gender journey—that would be impossible. But I hope you've gained some tools and spent some time reflecting so that you're able to fill in any blanks that pop up down the road. You don't need to have all the answers now or *ever*. I know that I don't, and I'm not itching to either. Once I figured out that I was nonbinary, it was off to the races. I did a speed-run of the typical transmasculine timeline, completing the medical and legal portions of my transition in under a year. I'm highly task-oriented, and I had access to gender-affirming healthcare, lived in California, and was in the early stages of a pandemic that left me with plenty of time to think through my thoughts and plan gender things out. But that wasn't the end for me. I still question how I'm doing gender all the time, and I like that. Gender journeys don't need to be fixed or linear, and there's something pretty freeing in that.

All this to say, I'm proud of you, excited for you, and so grateful you're here. I hope you're exiting this chapter of the book with a newfound sense of agency and thrill. I hope you'll get to look back on the notes you wrote today in many months and see how far you've come. Gather and utilize your support networks, make a plan, follow through on it at a pace that works for you, and let me know how it goes. You've got this, you deserve this, and you're going to do amazing things—with your gender and otherwise.

CHAPTER 9

A Mother's Point of View!

Are you ready to shift gears toward supporting others through their gender journeys? Chapter 8 laid out five suggestions for individuals who are navigating gender on their own, and Chapters 9 and 10 are specifically for the readers who are here to learn more about supporting their loved ones and other non-cis people they encounter. If you're an ally or an advocate here to learn more about gender advocacy, I'd like to briefly offer my thanks. Thank you for taking the initiative to be here and for agreeing to take some of the burden of education off the TGNCNB individuals in your life.

Before we get into my recommendations, examples, and practice material, I'd like to give someone else a chance to share their perspective: my mom. To be completely transparent: for the work we're doing in these next two chapters, I'm not necessarily the most helpful person to ask. In this context, I *am* the loved one in need of support, not the ally looking to *support* the loved one. To make sure we cover the angle I can't reach on my own, we're going to turn to my mother to hear her point of view as the woman who's had a front row seat to my gender journey thus far.

I'd like to introduce you to Gina, a biracial Black cis lesbian, a gospel singer and tambourinist from Ohio, and a catcher who still slides into the bases even though she's in her late fifties. My mother is *exactly* the person you'd picture to have raised me, and she can offer you a first-hand account of what it's been like to support me through my gender journey thus far. Enjoy.

OAKLEY: First, how would you describe my gender?

GINA: As nonbinary, encompassing both, and seeking life somewhere in the middle. I make a point of telling people that your gender identity is expressed daily, depending on how you wish to present yourself that day.

OAKLEY: That's pretty accurate! Next, how did you feel when I first told you I wanted to change my name?

GINA: Since I'd given you a name that represented a union [between me and your other mother] that no longer existed, I understood. At first, I thought "Oak" was kind of short, and it made me think of the tree, but I really love it now, and it reminds me of the strength you have in common with the tree.

OAKLEY: I'm glad that it really grew on you. It feels like it really fits me now. Next, and this may take us in a different direction, how have you found support as the parent of a genderqueer kid?

GINA: Well, I have a few close friends who listen intently, so that's where any of my confusion, frustration, or venting happens. You've also been very generous with sending me resources—blog posts and articles mostly—and I now use Google way more too.

OAKLEY: That makes sense. I'm grateful you have a few friends who've really tried to understand where we're both coming from. Next, though I'm fairly certain I already know your answer: what did you struggle with most when I came out as nonbinary, and what do you struggle with most today?

GINA: Same answer for both...your physical safety.

OAKLEY: Yep, that's what I was expecting you to say. What could I have done differently to support you during my coming outprocess?

GINA: Hmm. Being more patient with my process and understanding that while this had been something you'd been working on for a long time, it was also changing everything I'd known about you for your entire life.

OAKLEY: That's understandable. I was eager and a lot less patient back then. What could *you* have done differently to support me in my coming out process?

GINA: This is a hard one, because I feel like I adjusted to a *lot* in a relatively short amount of time. I probably could have given more effort sooner with your pronouns.

OAKLEY: That's true. Once you started really trying to pick it up, it was a quick change, but it took a while for us to get there... What surprised you most about my transition?

GINA: How different you look and sound, yet I somehow still see *you* in there.

OAKLEY: That's sweet! I said something similar to that a lot early on... "I'm still me." What questions about my gender do you still have for me?

GINA: Have you reached your "final destination," if there is such a thing? You seem happy, but is there anything you wouldn't have done, or done differently?

OAKLEY: I'm happy with where I'm at for now. There may be some changes down the line, but I don't see anything major coming up for a long while. Next, what positive and negative feedback do you receive the most when you explain me and my gender to the people in your life?

GINA: Ironically, the positive feedback always relates to how well *I'm* handling all this—which feels kind of negative too, because it's dismissive of all you've gone through. I've had some people want me to be more demanding in saying "no" to things, and I've had to explain that that isn't how you deal with a child who's over 18, in college, and lives in a different state. Ultimately, I tell them that they can love their child, or *lose* their child, so they have to figure that part out.

OAKLEY: What advice would you give to parents and guardians of newly out genderqueer kids?

GINA: To read your article in *Psychology Today*—shameless plug—and go to therapy! Therapy not to try and change the situation, but to have access to a professional who's trained in the field, someone who can help make sense of each person's perspective and where they're at in their own process.

OAKLEY: Absolutely. How would you like to see parenting change when it comes to supporting genderqueer youth?

GINA: I would love to live in a world where gender isn't immediately thrust on children at birth. Since your process began, I've had my eyes opened to how many things are ridiculously and unnecessarily gendered. I'd also like to see more support groups for parents of young children.

OAKLEY: As my mom, did it help that you were already living proudly under the LGBTQ+ label yourself when I came out as nonbinary?

GINA: Absolutely. It gave me some idea of the internal struggles you might've been going through.

OAKLEY: Makes sense! Anything else you'd like to add?

GINA: I love you. You're the best thing I ever did, and I'm ridiculously proud of you. Thank you for letting me be a part of your journey—which I love for you!

This interview has been edited for clarity and conciseness.

EXERCISE 7

Which questions from Oakley and Gina's interview would you like to ask your loved one/s?

. . . .

. . . .

. . . .

Which of your loved ones did you have in mind as you read the interview?

. . . .

. . . .

. . . .

If there was one thing you'd want your loved one/s to understand most of all in relation to gender, what would it be?

. . . .

. . . .

. . . .

CHAPTER 10

How Can I Support My Loved One Through Their Gender Journey?

W e're going to have some fun with this! For this section, nearly every piece of advice comes with an example and a few practice prompts. Let's make sure you and your loved ones have an easier time working through gender than Gina and I did. These recommendations for providing assistance and encouragement can work for any individual in your life who's trans, gender non-conforming, nonbinary, genderqueer, questioning, or any other form of not-cis. We're talking family members, friends, partners, co-workers, anyone in need of some gender affirmation!

Make sure to address your loved one by their chosen name, pronouns, and associated titles

It's your responsibility to put in the effort and make sure you're getting these words right, ranging from names to titles (son, partner, Mx., etc.). Your loved one deserves to be addressed in the ways that are most affirming for them, and this is an easy way to demonstrate your respect and care for them by trying your absolute hardest.

SCENARIO
Taylor (they/them/theirs) is Emily's kid. They're a gender-queer 17-year-old who was assigned male at birth. They're going to spend some time at the park with their male-identifying friends from high school.

>   DON'T: "The boys are on their way to the park."

>   DO: "Taylor and their friends are on their way to the park."

Can you tell what's wrong with the first statement?
If you guessed that the issue was that Taylor was subtly mis-gendered in the first statement, then you were correct. Taylor was lumped in with the boys, even though they're genderqueer and don't identify with that label. Make sure you're cognizant of how easy it is to slip up and misgender others, especially when you're discussing a group. Please make sure you're on your A-game when it comes to addressing your loved ones.

The amount of effort *you* put into correctly labeling your loved one directly correlates to how much effort *others* think they need to put in. Lead by example, and you'll be golden.

PRONOUN PRACTICE

- SUBJECT: they
- OBJECT: them
- POSSESSIVE: their/s
- REFLEXIVE: themself

Example: Taylor is great at skateboarding, and *they* (subject) are going to start offering classes this summer.

1. Taylor is holding onto _____ (possessive) skateboard.

2. When Taylor gets home from the park, _____ (subject) are going to make dinner.

Don't post or share any pre-transition photos of your loved one/s without their explicit consent

Make sure to ask before showing past pictures of your loved one to others or posting them on social media. The person in question should have the power to decide who's allowed to know how they looked before coming out and/or transitioning. If you're not cautious, you might accidentally out your loved one, and nobody wants that.

SCENARIO

Sonia (she/her/hers) has been the local librarian for the past ten years. She transitioned last winter and recently hired another assistant. When chatting with both of her assistants, they realize they'd all been in the same book club several years prior.

> DON'T: One of the assistants takes out his phone to search for an old photo of the book club. He finds it and shows the photo to everyone, unwittingly reminding people how Sonia presented before she transitioned.

> DO: One of the assistants takes out his phone to search for an old photo of the book club. He finds it and asks Sonia for approval before showing it to others.

Can you tell what's wrong with the first option?

I'm sure you picked up on the problem. Sonia needed to be consulted before that picture was shared in the library. If you've got pictures of a co-worker, friend, relative, classmate, or anybody else before they began presenting their gender as they do today, make sure to directly ask for their permission before you share.

How could you have supported Sonia in either of the two situations?

. . . .

. . . .

. . . .

Be mindful of how you tell pre-transition stories about your loved one

In addition to the previous tip about sharing images, sharing *stories* is also something to consider. Think about the pre-transition story you'd like to share. How is your loved one going to feel when they're reminded of this moment? Does the story feature another name or set of pronouns? Are you both in a safe environment to be able to share this story without any consequences?

SCENARIO

Max (he/him/his) is a ten-year-old trans boy. His dad, Arturo, is chatting with his friends about how great Max is at sports.

> DON'T: "Max is a triple threat—he plays soccer, he's learning tennis, and he's an outstanding swimmer! I do

wish she'd swim with the girls again. Her old relay team was unbeatable. Ever since Maxine came out as transgender, she swapped over to the boys' team in every sport she plays."

DO: "Max is a triple threat—he plays soccer, he's learning tennis, and he's an outstanding swimmer! He's working on improving his technique as the goalie for his new soccer team and he's making plenty of friends as well. Everyone wants to be best buds with the goalie!"

Can you see where Arturo went wrong in the first scenario?
In the first scenario, Arturo misgendered and deadnamed Max once he started picturing him with his old swim team before he came out as trans. In the second scenario, Arturo was more mindful and made sure to keep his focus on describing Max's life *today*. Make sure you're aware of the differences between the person in your story and the person you know now. If you don't think before you speak, you could trigger your loved one or out them in a potentially unsafe space. When in doubt, ask your loved one privately about the story, or just don't share it.

PRONOUN PRACTICE
- SUBJECT: he
- OBJECT: him
- POSSESSIVE: his

- REFLEXIVE: himself

1. Max wants to become a PE teacher when _____ (subject) grows up.

2. Arturo lets Max walk to school by _____ (reflexive) in the mornings.

Don't out your loved one

This one is self-explanatory.

Listen without centering yourself as much as possible

Your loved one's gender isn't about you, and it isn't yours either. That can sometimes be hard to conceptualize, but the sooner you can wrap your head around it, the better. Your feelings, concerns, and advice when it comes to your loved one's gender can all go other places, instead of onto that individual's shoulders. Therapy, journaling, and support groups can come in quite handy here. I want you to make sure you're also being supported, but that should never come at the expense of your loved one's mental health because they're already working through a *lot*.

SCENARIO

Egypt (she/they) is a transfeminine nonbinary young adult. Her mom, Michelle, is struggling to provide support because she doesn't have a support system of her own yet.

> **DON'T:** Michelle continues to ask Egypt invasive and uncomfortable questions about her coming out process and whether or not she plans to medically transition.

> **DO:** Michelle asks Egypt if she'd be comfortable explaining her gender to Michelle's best friend, Yvette. Egypt and Yvette get their nails done and sit in Yvette's car chatting after. After Egypt paints a beautiful picture of her gender to Yvette, all three of them work together to find a gender therapist for Egypt and a parents and guardians' support group for Michelle.

Can you tell what's different in the second option?

Egypt is now able to receive the support they need because their mom has gained access to other outlets for her more complicated feelings about gender that shouldn't necessarily be shared with her daughter. If you and yours aren't interested in or able to access therapy, asking a family friend or other trusted third party to get involved can be a helpful alternative. You don't specifically need a person with a degree to tell you that you shouldn't burden your loved ones with your emotions about *their* genders, but having an external figure who can serve as a sounding board while you sort out how best to care for your loved ones can help significantly. In other words, make sure everyone's got support from a few loving, listening ears.

Who could play Yvette's role in your current circumstances?

. . . .

. . . .

. . . .

Calmly correct others if they misgender or misname your loved one (if your loved one's out)

Your loved one can only be in one place at a time, I'm assuming. When they're not around, you're responsible for making sure they're being given respect. They need (and deserve) help in the ever-present fight for queer and trans visibility, inclusion, and access to gender-affirming care. If you hear misnaming, misgendering, or other misrepresentation of your loved one's identity, step in and say something, whether or not they're present, as long as you know that that's a safe and reasonable decision to make. If your loved one *isn't* out to the person misgendering them or that individual could be dangerous to argue with, give your choice an extra thought before you make it. I want you both to be safe—safety first, "the fight for change" second.

SCENARIO

Miya (they/them/theirs) works at the local coffee shop. Two weeks ago, they came out to their co-workers as gender non-conforming and shared that their pronouns are they/them/theirs. Almost all of Miya's co-workers are doing an excellent job respecting their identity—Nick is the only one struggling. Adrian gets a chance to step in when the three of them are on shift together.

DON'T: Adrian notices that Nick frequently misgenders Miya, and he sees the negative impact it's having on them. But Adrian doesn't think it's his place as a cis straight guy to correct Nick's behavior, so he doesn't say anything.

DO: Adrian notices that Nick frequently misgenders Miya, and he sees the negative impact it's having on them. When Miya leaves the counter to bring a drink to a customer sitting outside, Adrian takes this chance to briefly chat with Nick. He re-informs Nick of Miya's pronouns and offers to share links to the articles he read about the importance of respecting other people's personal pronouns. Nick agrees to read them when he finishes his shift.

What was different about Adrian's approach in the second scenario?

If your answer was that Adrian chose not to stay silent, you'd be correct. The second time, Adrian chose to step in instead of remaining beholden to his fear that he'd be stepping out of line if he took action. He also made a great choice by waiting until he was alone with Nick, so that Miya didn't have to be present for any confrontation. They didn't *have* to be there for advocacy and education to occur—allies can almost always share that burden. Adrian calmly corrected Nick and offered resources for further learning, which is ideal. If you ever end up in a similar position to Adrian, you've got this. Remember to always approach your corrections with love and with the hope that that person is doing their best.

PRONOUN PRACTICE

- SUBJECT: they
- OBJECT: them
- POSSESSIVE: their/s
- REFLEXIVE: themself

1. Miya enjoys catching up with _____ (possessive) customers.

2. Miya makes a matcha latte for _____ (reflexive) when they end _____ (possessive) shift.

Explore and question your own gender

This is a great time to look back at Chapter 4. Remember that? What were your answers when we began to think about your gender? If you're looking for more places to start, you can also head back to Chapter 7 for a quick list of gender-affirming recommendations to check out! Whenever possible, question what you think you know about gender, and open yourself up to new knowledge. Remember that gender isn't identical for any two people, and there are thousands upon thousands of different ways to understand it. The more you ask yourself the tough questions your loved one is trying to answer for themselves, the better prepared you'll be to help. Once you're able to see first-hand how much time and energy goes into a gender journey, you'll truly understand just how strong and wise your loved one really is.

Defend your loved one and their gender

Your loved one deserves all the support they can get, and that means you'll also need to stand up for them in front of others—defending them, validating their identity, and making sure not to let transphobia off the hook where you're forced to bear witness to it. If you've decided to be there for your loved one for the long haul, you'll need to get used to defending them as we all work to make gender inclusivity something fewer people need to "get on board with."

SCENARIO

Minnow (all) is an elementary school teacher, and they use any pronouns. Many of the teachers at Minnow's school are older and on the more conservative end, and they're refusing to support or welcome Minnow. Maliq, one of Minnow's students, overhears two teachers talking behind Minnow's back on his way to recess, and he has a choice to make about how he's going to respond.

DON'T: Maliq hears Mrs. Jones say, "Minnow likes to think she's special because she uses 'any pronouns.' She looks like every other girl," and Ms. Sparden say, "I'd be willing to bet her real name isn't Minnow either." This upsets Maliq because he likes having Minnow as his fourth-grade teacher, and he doesn't understand why the other teachers are being mean to them. But he wants to get to recess, so he keeps walking and pretends he didn't hear anything.

DO: Maliq hears Mrs. Jones say, "Minnow likes to think she's special because she uses 'any pronouns.' She looks like every other girl," and Ms. Sparden say, "I'd be willing to bet her real name isn't Minnow either." He continues toward recess but stops at his backpack first. Maliq pulls out a pen and his sketchpad and writes in bold purple letters: "TO MS. SPARDEN AND MRS. JONES: MINNOW IS NICE AND MINNOW IS NOT A GIRL. IT

IS MEAN TO CALL MINNOW SOMETHING THEY ARE NOT. YOU SHOULD SAY YOU ARE SORRY TO MINNOW AFTER SCHOOL TODAY." Maliq folds the note, hands it to Ms. Sparden, and then heads outside to enjoy the rest of recess on the jungle gym.

What do you think of Maliq's response?
Go Maliq! If Maliq can stand up for Minnow, you can stand up for the Minnows in your life too. You're fully capable of defending your non-cis loved ones, whether they're your partner, professor, student, friend, parent, co-worker, or anybody else. Be persistent, be calm, and above all, remember who you're doing this for.

What would you do if you were put into Maliq's position?

Commit to supporting all of the TGNCNB people in your life—beyond your loved one

If you came to this chapter, I'd imagine you're reading it with a specific person in mind, and I have full confidence that you're prepared to charge back into the world as an outstanding ally and advocate for that individual after finishing this section, and that's *excellent*, but that isn't the end of your work. If the only non-cis person you care about is the one you know, that isn't good enough. Your job goes beyond the people in your immediate circle. To give you an idea, here is some of the work that still needs to be done:

- Create and convert more gender-segregated restrooms into gender-neutral restrooms.
- Review institutional paperwork to make sure it's updated with gender-affirming language.
- Start every set of introductions with names and pronouns (to the extent people are comfortable sharing).
- Put funding into more gender-affirming spaces (GSAs, Pride contingents, equality, diversity and inclusion (EDI) committees, etc.).
- Make the process of socially and legally changing names and pronouns more accessible and cost-friendly.
- Get funding to individuals in need of gender-affirming surgeries on GoFundMe.
- Create more workshops, groups, and safe spaces dedicated to TGNCNB inclusion.

To be clear, I'm not expecting you to do all these things on your own. Pick a starting point that works with your school, workplace, team, congregation, and so on, and go from there.

Anything you can do to make the spaces you inhabit safer for non-cis individuals is going to help. I believe in you, and I know you're capable of doing this work and extending your advocacy beyond your own loved one. There are too many TGNCNB people in need of basic safety and support services. We need more people doing this work—why shouldn't it be you? Why *couldn't* it be you? Get out there and start making gender-affirming waves. You've got me here as your gender friend to help cheer you on.

EXERCISE 8

Which scenario was easiest for you to relate to? Hardest?

. . . .

. . . .

. . . .

What did you take away from seeing how each scenario shifted from "DON'T" to "DO?"

. . . .

. . . .

. . . .

Which larger gender advocacy project (creating
gender-neutral restrooms, reviewing and updating
paperwork, etc.) could you work on?

. . . .

. . . .

. . . .

CHAPTER 11

What Not to Say

Let's check in! How are you doing? Have you had any water recently? Are you reading in a comfortable position? Have you had a moment to breathe today? If you didn't like your answer to any of those questions, set the book down and go address those needs. I'll still be here.

All better? Awesome. We're nearing the end of our time together, but don't worry! We've still got a few loose ends to tie up. Now that we know how to support ourselves and others through their gender journeys, let's take some time to lay out exactly what we shouldn't be doing. When it comes to affirming others and lifting them up, sometimes, what we don't do is as important as what we are doing.

This section has a variety of statements and questions I've either heard directed at me or at other transmasculine individuals. I'm going to break down precisely what's wrong with them and why they're statements better left unsaid.

* * *

THEY SAID: *Are you going to fully transition?*
THEY MEANT: *Are you going to transition in a way that I can understand?*

There are two ways this question can go: (1) bottom surgery, and (2) binary transitions. First, bottom surgery is private, and it doesn't make or break a transition. Claiming that a "full transition" must end in a change of genitals is false, and it excludes individuals who don't want or can't access bottom surgery. All gender journeys are valid, regardless of where they start or end. And second, a transition isn't less valid if it's in relation to being nonbinary. Binary trans men and women are as important as nonbinary individuals—we're all just trying to get to a place in our gender journeys where we feel content. Claiming that a transition is incomplete is never an outsider's place, and "completing" a transition is rarely, if ever, the point.

* * *

THEY SAID: *What's your deadname?*
THEY MEANT: *What's your real name?*

A deadname, or a birth name that's been changed, is no longer in use for a reason. There are few cases in which an individual is obligated to share the name they were given at birth, and those situations are usually based in legal "necessity." It's highly unlikely that a person who's changed their name will share their old name with you, unless you've earned their trust and they've got a good reason to tell you. Deadnames are dead for a reason, and it's best to leave them in the past where they belong. If we want to share them, we will—otherwise, you can pretend our birth names never existed.

* * *

THEY SAID: *Which bathroom do you use?*
THEY MEANT: *What's in your pants?*

This is not a question that needs to be answered. Unless your intent is to know which bathroom I plan on using so that you can keep a lookout for me and make sure I return safely, you don't need to know. Any answer to that question shouldn't change how you treat any TGNCNB person. The "bathroom issue" is a small part of what non-cis individuals are forced to contend with on a daily basis, and this question is invasive and unlikely to be received warmly. In short, you don't need to know what's in anyone's pants in order to treat them with dignity.

* * *

THEY SAID: *What happens if you change your mind?*
THEY MEANT: *I don't think you're making the right decision.*

If a person on a gender journey decides that they want to undo, pause, or change their plans in any way, that isn't necessarily them realizing they've "made the wrong decision." De-transitioning can occur, and that is sometimes the best choice for individuals who've realized that transitioning wasn't the solution that worked best for them, but this is only one possibility. Instead of asking your loved one to make a back-up plan in case their current strategy doesn't work out, ask them an affirming question. You could ask about their new name, what clothing they'd like from the store, how you could support them financially, or something as simple as asking how they're doing. Save negative or stressful questions for the gender therapists.

* * *

THEY SAID: *Why don't you come home more often?*
THEY MEANT: *Why isn't home good enough for you anymore?*

I don't go back to my hometown more than twice a year if I can avoid it. It's a small town, and I was decently well known there (as Jordan). I don't feel safe there as Oakley, my authentic self, because the demure, hypersexualized young woman who left my town isn't me anymore. I don't fit into the small world of my small town, and I stand out like a sore thumb when I go back and dress in my usual queer attire. In short, I don't come home more because home doesn't feel like home anymore, and that scenario is true for too many queer and trans people. Rather than asking this question, make the journey to visit us or schedule a call instead.

* * *

THEY SAID: *I don't get it.*
THEY MEANT: *I don't care enough to try.*

I can't stress this strongly enough: no one is incapable of understanding gender if they're willing to put in the effort. I know that almost all of us were raised against the backdrop of the gender binary, and I know that that screwed up most of us in niche and nuanced ways, but we *can* break out of it. Unlearning is hard work, but, if you care enough to be here reading this, I guarantee you're on the right track. The non-cis people in your life deserve your best efforts, and I have every confidence that you can become an outstanding gender advocate if you commit and put in the time.

* * *

THEY SAID: *You're rejecting your womanhood.*
THEY MEANT: *You're denying your womanhood in order to identify as transmasculine.*

It took some time for me to understand that part of why I

medically transitioned was so that I could reclaim my femininity from an angle that actually worked for me. I'd grown tired of being perceived as a young woman, and I knew that T and top surgery would make presenting in a way that aligned more closely with "young effeminate man" more accessible for me as an AFAB. Now, I can show my femininity from a fun, backroads angle, without my gender being misinterpreted and misunderstood. Essentially, now I can wear skirts and makeup again and still be gendered correctly. Surprisingly, I'm still pretty femme, and I'm happy with that. When I received this comment, it cut deep because I knew just how wrong it was. Please don't tell your loved one that they're denying X or Y part of themselves—you have absolutely no way of knowing that.

* * *

THEY SAID: *You want to be a boy.*
THEY MEANT: *I want you to be a boy, because that would be easier for me to understand.*

When I came out as nonbinary, I heard this sentiment frequently. I remember being told that it'd be easier if I were a trans man, because that would "make more sense" than being nonbinary—which boiled down to that person telling me that it'd be easier for them if my gender meant that they didn't need to do any extra work. It isn't helpful to tell any non-cis person that their gender is too hard or complicated for you. That's not your place to decide. It *is* your job to get educated and to make sure that you're equipped to properly care for the person that your loved one is, not the person you wish they'd be.

* * *

THEY SAID: *You don't seem different.*
THEY MEANT: *You don't look different, so I can't separate the person I knew from the person you're becoming.*

Medically transitioning isn't a prerequisite for being non-cis. Transitioning in a way that the outsider can see isn't necessarily what every TGNCNB individual wants. There are plenty of non-cis people who aren't on HRT or undergoing procedures, and that can be for any number of reasons—personal, interpersonal, and/or institutional. When someone comes out as a different gender than what had previously been attributed to them, that's all they need to verbalize. They don't need to change anything about their presentation for their gender to be valid, and they definitely don't need to perfectly align with how you were expecting them to change. Anyone can be any gender, and any gender can look however it wants. Refer back to Chapter 7 for more information on how gender attribution needs to be broken down. Know that for every description of a nonbinary person, man, or woman, that same description can fit for another gender. The boxes we've assigned to different genders are arbitrary, and they're easily able to be disproved.

* * *

THEY SAID: *You keep asking for more.*
THEY MEANT: *Why can't you be happy with where you're at in your journey?*

When I told Gina I was nonbinary, I didn't tell her that I want-ed to start T or have top surgery, because *I* didn't know that yet. All I knew for sure was that I wasn't a girl—everything else was still so new and so overwhelming that I couldn't have tackled it all at once. When I later came to Gina with the updated plan to medically transition if our insurance could help cover it, she wasn't thrilled that I'd changed my tune. I understood her frustration with having to wrap her head around a changing plan, but I also understood that I couldn't possibly have known everything in advance. There aren't many how-to books for being not-cis, so we have to do most of the work in the beginning on our own. To my allies reading, don't assume that your loved one's gender journey will be linear with clearly defined starts and stops. It's rarely ever that simple, and that's okay.

* * *

All this is to say that there are questions and comments that non-cis people are pretty tired of hearing. The biggest thing to remember is that your non-cis loved ones aren't here to educate you or defend themselves to you, and you don't need to perfectly understand every part of their identities in order to be able to respect, love, and support them. Many of these questions are better suited to Google searches, gender therapists, support groups, or simply to being left unsaid.

But let's not end this section on the negatives. Instead of using the questions or comments we unpacked above, try any of these instead:

- "I'm so happy for you!"
- "Let me know if you'd ever like me to walk with you to the restrooms and wait outside."
- "Do you want me to help you look for an affirming hair stylist or clothing store?"
- "Thanks for sharing your identity with me. How can I best support you?"
- "Do you feel safe visiting home for the holidays, or would you like me to come to you?"
- "Do you want me to start researching how to get your name changed at school/work?"
- "Is there anything you'd like me to watch or read to learn more about your gender?"
- "Are there any names you'd like me to try using for you?"
- "I'm here for you, however you'd like me to be."

If you make an effort to think before you speak and correct yourself when you mess up, you'll do well. Being an ally isn't about being perfect; it's about working as hard as you can to get educated and keep yourself that way. You've got this, and as your gender friend, I know you're ready now to be able to support your questioning and non-cis loved ones through anything they may face.

EXERCISE 9

Which statements or questions did you recognize?

. . . .

. . . .

. . . .

Are there any statements or questions you'd add to this list?

. . . .

. . . .

. . . .

Write down three words that describe how you'd like to feel when you're approached, or when you approach others, with gender-related questions (for example, safe, supported, welcomed).

. . . .

. . . .

. . . .

CHAPTER 12

Putting It All Together!

N eed more deep breaths? A water break? A quick dance break? There is *always* time for a quick dance break! I'll wait. I'll be here grooving...okay, let's keep going. Look at how far we've come. We've questioned, explored, analyzed, unpacked, opened up, and improved our knowledge of gender. We've covered every learning objective I set for us, and all that's left to do now is to put it all together into something you can easily remember. How many of us have read outstanding, life-changing books, sworn that they'd change the way we lived our lives forever, and then forgot what they said after a few months? Well, we don't want that to happen here, and we're going to avoid it with a simple acronym: *VASE* (*Variety, Assumption, Support, and Experience*). You can remember a vase, right? Scribble it down on a sticky note, get a vase tattooed on your ankle, buy a vase from Goodwill and put it on your nightstand—anything that'll help keep that acronym in your mind for the long haul.

Now, let's explain what *VASE* means.

V is for Variety. It's meant to remind you that there is no one-size-fits-all for gender journeys. As your gender friend, I've given you an intimate look into my gender timeline, and I can guarantee that it's uncommon for a non-cis individual to complete the logistics of their gender journey in under a year, like I did. I was able to legally and medically transition in under a year because I had access to insurance, lived in the Pacific Northwest, and had Gina's support. If any of those factors had been missing, it would've taken substantially longer for me to change my name, start HRT, and have top surgery—in fact, it would've taken years longer.

I can't express strongly enough that gender journeys are complicated, and they aren't linear. My gender journey also isn't over, by any means. I'm going to be taking testosterone for the foreseeable future—until I have a mustache and a beard (because my 25 chin hairs and faint mustache ain't cutting it), and I might consider bottom surgery in the future too. Outside of my medical transition, I know that my gender will continue to evolve naturally over time as I continue to explore and question what I know and like. I never want to reach a point where my gender feels locked into place, and I'm sure many feel similarly about their goals to continuously play with their gender presentations, learn more about their bodies as they relate to gender, and re-assess how they've come to understand their gender identities. When your aim is to feel as safe and at home in your body as you can, that's likely to be a long-term project for any person, cis or not. Every gender journey deserves respect as it occurs on the timeline that works for each individual.

A is for Assumption. Don't assume that you know other people's genders better than they do. The most frequent way assumption manifests is in gender attribution, the audio and visual cues we use to assume another person's gender. For me, at least, it feels nearly impossible to fully shut off that part of my brain, but it's something that you and I can at least work against. A quick fix is using they/them/theirs pronouns for everyone unless told otherwise. That removes a large part of where others can get hurt. It's imperative to remember that anyone can be any gender, regardless of what you may think they should be based on their appearance. That concept extends beyond the nonbinary and/or trans people in your immediate social circles. Your barista, nurse, cashier, Uber driver, and so on—any person you interact with—could be any gender under the sun, so not assuming is something to be worked on at all hours of the day. As long as you introduce yourself with your name and pronouns and invite others to do the same, you can circumvent much of the problem before it starts.

S is for Support. Therapists, support groups, Facebook groups, WhatsApp group chats, YouTube channels, TikToks, blogs, Instagram comment sections—any place where you can interact with people who have similar circumstances will do. If there isn't a space built specifically for questioning and non-cis people near you, start one. You can do it. You can be the person who begins building that outlet, and you hopefully won't have to work on it alone for long. A weekly book club, a monthly meet-up at a coffee shop or bar, or a Discord server are all great places to start. You by no means have to start a fully fledged Pride parade or drag show in your town, unless you have the bandwidth for that, in which case, go off! At the end of the day, just make sure you and yours and them and theirs all have someplace safe to turn to for gender support.

E is for Experience. The more time you spend working with gender, the better you'll get at learning what is and isn't affirming. If you put in the effort to keep educating yourself and entering into spaces where you can be educated without putting undue burden onto others (workshops, books, lectures, etc.), you'll keep growing in your ability to be an ally or gender advocate. If you chose to be here reading this text, I'm confident that you truly care and want to continue to deepen your knowledge as the movement for gender inclusivity continues to gather steam.

And that is *VASE* (*Variety, Assumption, Support, Experience*). That should alleviate the stress of trying to memorize every piece of this text, because that isn't realistic. My hope is that you'll turn to this book when you need it, and that you'll share it with others or recommend it to them as you see fit. I'm sure you'll pass on the "gender friend" message, and I hope that you'll surpass the knowledge laid out in this text. In fact, I'm sure you will. At the time of writing, I'm only 20 years old, and I came out as genderqueer a little over two years ago. I've got tons of learning to do that can't and won't be captured in this book. I hope we both can take this text as a jumping-off point for the work that is to come.

It's Been a Pleasure
and an Honor

When you walked into this book, what did you expect to learn? Well, nobody walked into it...when you *opened up* this book, what were you hoping for? Did you get some answers? Some better questions to ask? Some more appropriate words to use for your loved ones? An intimate understanding of a genderqueer person's story? I hope that you're walking away from this book (closing it) with a sense of "I've got this." You showed up, put some hours in, and completed this text. That's pretty rad. Your job now is to take what you've learned and apply it, to make your gender journey and the gender journeys of the people in your vicinity a little easier.

Knowing what I hope you've learned, I also hope that you felt safe and cared for as you read this text. When I move through the world, I always feel unsafe. I am constantly modifying how I present myself, how I dress, walk, talk, and sit to improve my chances of safety. Being Black, trans, queer, and nonbinary in the States isn't pleasant; it's demoralizing. I hope you didn't feel that way as you read. I hope you felt seen, heard, respected, and supported, and I'm sure that, after reading, you know how important it is to make sure others feel those same ways when they're approaching gender with a critical eye for the first time.

I'd also like to briefly acknowledge that this text isn't going to become a monolith. It shouldn't. There isn't a gender resource out there like *The Gender Friend* yet, but there will be work that comes after this text and expands upon it. I know that this book will become situated in the context of the early 2020s, and I'm content with that. We just need something more modern to build from. I hope this text can fill that gap, and I also can't wait to see where gender goes next.

And with that, we've reached the end. I want to leave you with these thoughts. Turn them into mantras, write them on sticky notes, send them to your loved ones, or simply let them sink in in this moment.

You are valid.

Your gender is valid.

You deserve as much gender euphoria as you can possibly get your hands on.

You are not alone in the mess that is navigating the systemic gender binary.

You are more than capable of breaking free of the gender binary, in big ways and little ways every day.

Thank you for showing up to do this work. As my friend Garrett would say, it's been a pleasure and an honor. I hope you'll write to *orphoenixtheauthor@gmail.com* and keep me posted. I'd love to hear from you. Now, go out there and show your gender who's boss.

With love,

Oakley "Oak" Phoenix
The Gender Friend

Acknowledgments

To Cannon, Garrett, Melodie, Silver, Avenue, Danielle, and Alia, and the many others from Willamette who've been there for me since the earliest days of me questioning my gender up until now. I changed your names to maintain your privacy, but I'm sure you all know who you are. I want each of you to know that I wouldn't be Oakley without your encouragement and support over these last two years. Your listening ears, the moments where you pointed out the obvious things that I'd been missing, your willingness to try different names and pronouns for me until I settled into myself, your continued creation of safe spaces for me to grow and flourish, and your hugs. I cannot thank you enough. You all are incredible.

To Gina, you've been there for me, and you've looked out for me largely on your own, for as long as I can remember. We've had our ups and downs over the years, but I'm elated to see where our relationship is now. You continue to show me that a Baby Boomer is never past the age of learning and committing to do better. You've loved me unconditionally on my journey, and I love you with all of my heart, Mom.

To Jessica Kingsley Publishers, thank you for this opportunity. I hadn't entered into the summer of 2021 expecting to write a book. I'd been expecting to start my junior year of college, and receiving the email from Andrew, JKP's Editorial Director, in July was a surprise to say the least. Writing and editing *The Gender Friend* over the course of the first half of my junior year of undergrad was a challenge, but I wouldn't have had it any other way. I'm grateful my words can reach a broader audience of people, non-cis and cis alike, who are in need of a "gender friend" who can make 102 Gender theory more approachable and exciting. Thank you for taking a chance on me, and I hope to work with the JKP family again someday.

To my partner, Ryder, who kept this project a secret for nearly half a year. At the time of writing, they were the only person besides me and JKP who knew this experience was taking place, and they never let the secret slip. To this day, I don't know how they did it. Ryder, thank you for supporting me as a new author and as the human ball of anxiety I am the rest of the time. I hope you know that you (and Twig) have made my life better in immeasurable ways, and I'm glad to be your "golden retriever" goofball every day. I love you, bucko.

To the readers, thank you for grabbing my book off the shelf. I'm honored that you took the time to get to know me and my story, and I hope you feel a connection to this text. I want you to feel seen and supported and ready to take on the world, and I have every bit of confidence that you'll do just that. If we ever cross paths off the page, I hope I get to give you a fist-bump.

And lastly, to every questioning, trans, gender non-conforming, and/or nonbinary person reading this, I'm glad you're still here. Existing is hard, and everything we do on a daily basis to take care of ourselves in a world that doesn't seem to care is exhausting. Every moment we spend existing happily is a mini revolution, even though it doesn't always feel that way. I hope the ones who come after us will have an easier time because of the work we do each day, just as the ones who came before us held that hope for us. You are beautiful, you are good enough, and you are going to get through this. You are everything you need to be and more, and you're exactly the person your younger self needed. Be proud of yourself. Be proud of us. You are wondrous, and I can't wait to see what we do together next.

Take care.

Further Reading

"Definitions." (2020, 15 April).
TSER (Trans Student Educational Resources).

"Frequently Asked Questions about Transgender People."
(2016, 9 July). National Center for Transgender Equality.

"Gender Wiki." Gender Wiki/Fandom.

Jussim, L. (2019, 20 March). "Rapid onset gender
dysphoria." *Psychology Today*, Sussex Publishers.

"PFLAG National Glossary of Terms." (2021, January). PFLAG.

Price, D. (2018, 16 November). "Gender Socialization
Is Real (Complex)." Medium, Medium.

Russo, J. (2014). The Queer Dictionary.

"Transgender FAQ." (2021, 11 January). GLAAD.

Index

They/Them/Their
A Guide to Nonbinary and Genderqueer Identities
Eris Young

£18.99 | $26.95 | PB | 288PP |
ISBN 978 1 78592 483 5 |
eISBN 978 1 78450 872 2

In this insightful and long-overdue book, Eris Young explores what it's like to live outside of the gender binary and how it can impact on one's relationships, sense of identity, use of language and more.

Drawing on the author's own experiences as a nonbinary person, as well as interviews and research, *They/Them/Their* shares common experiences and challenges faced by those who are nonbinary, and what friends, family and other cisgender people can do to support them. Breaking down misconceptions and providing definitions, information on healthcare, the history of nonbinary identities and gender-neutral language, this much-needed guide is for anyone wanting to fully understand nonbinary and genderqueer identities.

Eris Young is a queer, nonbinary trans writer and editor from Santa Ana, California, and currently lives in Edinburgh, UK.

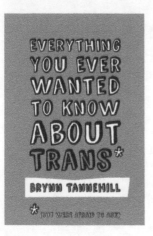

Everything You Ever Wanted to Know about Trans (But Were Afraid to Ask)

Brynn Tannehill

£14.99 | $21.95 | PB | 432PP | ISBN 978 1 78592 826 0 | eISBN 978 1 78450 956 9

Breaking down misconceptions about trans people across all aspects of life, from politics and culture, religion and mental health, this book provides readers with a deeper understanding of what it means to be trans. It asks "What does transgender mean?" before moving on to more complex topics such as growing up trans, dating and sex, medical issues, and arguments around gender and feminism. Transphobic myths are debunked and biased research, bad statistics, and bad science are carefully and clearly refuted.

Brynn Tannehill is a leading trans activist and essayist, and has written for The New York Times, The Huffington Post, Bilerico, Slate, Salon, USA Today, The Advocate, LGBTQ Nation, The New Civil Rights Movement, as a blogger and featured columnist.

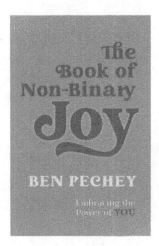

The Book of Non-Binary Joy
Embracing the Power of You
Ben Pechey
Illustrated by Sam Prentice

£12.99 | $18.95 | PB | 224PP |
ISBN 978 1 78775 910 7 |
eISBN 978 1 78775 911 4

'Oh hello darling, and welcome to *The Book of Non-Binary Joy*! This book is here to help you be yourself – free from judgement and expectation – as you unlock more joy in your life. Take my hand, and let's start your journey of self-love today.'

Whether you are at the start of your journey or have been on the wild ride of gender introspection for a long time, this guide is here to help you thrive as your authentic – and most fabulous – non-binary self. With personal stories, valuable insights and interactive sections, this inspiring book covers a wide range of topics, including mental health, pleasure, fashion, understanding your past, allyship privilege and self-expression. Written with warmth and unapologetic humour, and with bold illustrations throughout, Ben Pechey has created the ultimate safe space for you to embrace your non-binary life and start living.

Ben Pechey is a non-binary writer, presenter and fashion icon. They have written and produced content for *The Guardian*, *Cosmopolitan*, *Women's Health*, *Refinery29* and worked with a range of leading brands to educate and improve awareness of the LGBTQIA+ community. *The Book of Non-Binary Joy* is their first book.

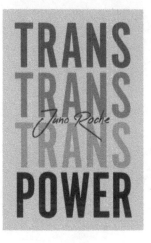

Trans Power
Own Your Gender
Juno Roche

£14.99 | $20.95 | PB | 256PP |
ISBN 978 1 78775 019 7|
eISBN 978 1 78775 020 3

'All those layers of expectation which are thrust upon us – boy, masculine, femme, transgender, sexual, woman, real – are such a weight to carry around. I feel transgressive. I feel hybrid. I feel trans.'

In this radical and emotionally raw book, Juno Roche pushes the boundaries of trans representation by redefining 'trans' as an identity with its own power and strength, that goes beyond the gender binary.

Through intimate conversations with leading and influential figures in the trans community, such as Kate Bornstein, Travis Alabanza, Josephine Jones, Glamrou and E-J Scott, this book highlights the diversity of trans identities and experiences with regard to love, bodies, sex, race and class, and urges trans people – and the world at large – to embrace a 'trans' identity as something that offers empowerment and autonomy. Powerfully written, this is essential reading for anyone interested in the future of gender and how we identify ourselves.

Juno Roche is an internationally recognised trans writer and campaigner. She featured on *The Independent's* Rainbow List 2015 and 2016, she is a director of cliniQ and received the 2015 NUT Blair Peach Award for her campaign 'Why Trans Teachers Matter'. She regularly contributes to publications including *Bitch*, *Dazed*, *The Guardian* and *Vice* and is the author of *Queer Sex*.